NOTHING
IMPOSSIBLE

CHAPLAIN
GLENN E. DAVIS

The story of the Chaplain's ministry at the Fresno County Jail and how God changed hardened criminals, drug addicts and gang members into useful citizens, pastors and more.

This book has a two-fold purpose...

...to help those who do not know Christ as their Lord and Savior to come to Him and learn to know Him.

...to encourage and strengthen those who do know Him as their Lord and Savior.

My deepest thanks...

...to my friend, Glendon Bender. Without his encouragement I would never have written this book.

...to my son, Brent, whose insightful suggestions and help in compiling this book were extremely beneficial.

...to Myrna, my wife of over 65 years, without whose love and support my jail ministry would not have been possible.

This book...

...is dedicated to the many volunteers who made our jail ministry possible. One year we had 68 volunteers; a few came once a month, most once a week, and a number came in several times a week. THANK YOU ALL!

- CONTENTS -

- INTRODUCTION -

My Grandfather Wilkinson died when I was seven years old. Though that has been over 75 years ago I remember it quite clearly. I remember my Mother crying profusely, though his death did not greatly affect me, until my Dad told some friends, "It will happen to all of us someday." What! Some day I would be lying there all cold and still like Grandfather. Fear gripped my heart. Three years later I found the answer to my fear.

When I was ten years old and living in Bridgeville, California, I received Christ as my personal Lord and Savior. This was the answer to my fear of death and it started me on a wonderful journey that eventually led me to jail...as a chaplain.

My father, Roy Davis, was chairman of the local school board. A Reverend Max Stowe wanted to hold a Vacation Bible School (VBS) in the schoolhouse during Christmas vacation in 1940. He came to my father to get permission to use the school house for a week.

When my older sister, Mary (she was 13, almost 14 and knew everything!), told me that this Reverend Stowe was going to hold a week of Vacation Bible School at the schoolhouse, I asked her, "What is Vacation Bible School?" She replied, "It is something like church." I then asked, "What is church?"

During the week of VBS Reverend Stowe told us the story of Daniel and made clear that we could be saved and have eternal life by trusting Christ as our Lord and Savior. He told us how Christ died for us to pay for our sins and then rose again from the grave. He explained that if we would trust Christ as our Savior He would forgive us of our sins, give us eternal life and we would go to heaven when we died.

At the end of the week he gave an invitation to accept

Christ as our Savior. He asked us to bow our heads in prayer and that if we wanted to receive Christ as Savior to raise our hand and he would lead us in a prayer of commitment. I wanted to do that more than anything in the world because I knew that this was the answer to my fear of death, but I said to myself, "I am not going to go first." (Why I thought that I don't know.) Just then I heard my other sister, Louise, praying to trust Christ. I couldn't wait for her to finish her prayer and get my hand up. I prayed the prayer that Rev. Stowe told me to pray and Christ became my Savior.

As we left the schoolhouse my friend, Gene, gave me a shove and said, "Ol' Glenn is getting to be a sissy." I wouldn't have cared if he had hit me. I had a warm feeling in the pit of my stomach and I KNEW that my sins were forgiven and that I was saved.

However, I did have a couple of wrong ideas as a ten-year-old Christian: one, I thought that now that I was saved that I would never sin again. But I did! Then I thought that I was now lost forever. But I wasn't! God is good. The Holy Spirit showed me a verse in the Bible, John 3:36. This verse says in the King James Version, **"He that believeth on the Son hath everlasting life: and he that believeth not the Son shall not see life; but the wrath of God abideth on him."** (KJV)

As I read that verse I remember saying to myself, "Whatever it means to believe in Jesus, I believe, therefore I have everlasting life." At the time I didn't realize it, but I had just learned an important lesson: God said it, I believe it, that settles it.

The summer of 1947, when I was sixteen years old, I attended a summer Bible camp at Mt. Lassen in Northern California. This camp was conducted by Reverend Gordon Titus, a missionary with what was then called the American Sunday School Union. The speaker was Dr. Lowell Wendt, who later became my pastor in Los Angeles. That first night, as we all sat around a campfire, Rev. Wendt gave a message. I do not recall his message, but as he gave an invitation for anyone to come forward and dedicate their lives to Christ, I responded.

My counselor, Bill Adams, was a student from the Bible Institute of Los Angeles (Biola) and I was greatly impressed with his devotion to Christ. The next morning he asked me if I had ever thought about going to Bible school. I hadn't; I didn't even know what Bible school was. When he told me about Biola, I said to him, "Bill, is that where you go?" When he responded, "Yes," I said, "Then I am going to Biola, too."

The rest, as they say, is history. When I graduated from high school in 1948 I entered Biola. There I met my wife, Myrna Maxwell, and we were married on May 13, 1952. In 1955 our only child, a son, Brent, was born. In January of 1956 we left to go to the state of Washington as rural missionaries with an organization called Student Missionary Council.

In the Fall of 1956 I was called to pastor the Little Stone Church in Chelan, Washington. After four years there we moved to Roseburg, Oregon, where I was pastor of Melrose Community Church, which was just outside of Roseburg. In 1967, I was called to my third and final pastorate at Staub Memorial Congregational Church in Portland, Oregon.

Because Myrna could not stand the cold, damp weather in Oregon, we realized we needed to move to a warmer climate so, in 1974, we moved to Fresno, California. We found hot weather! It was 113 degrees one day in Fresno.

For a time I worked as a chaplain with the Hospital Chaplains' Ministry of America (now Healthcare Chaplains' Ministry of America). I served at Valley Medical Center and Beverly Manor Convalescent Hospital, both in Fresno. It was at Valley Medical Center that I met Reverend Russell Knight who was the head chaplain at the Fresno County Jail. And that is where this book begins.

This book is about the power of God to transform lives through His Holy Spirit as He works through the Word of God, the Bible. The setting is the Fresno County Jail in

Fresno, California, but the principles used in the chaplains' ministry there will work anywhere.

In the book I will only use first names except in some of the cases where ex-inmates have shared their testimonies and obviously wish their full name to be used. In some cases I have changed the names in order to protect the privacy of individuals.

Remember the verse God gave me as a ten-year-old boy? Here it is in the New Living Translation (NLT). The Bible–the Book of Truth–says: **"And all who believe in God's Son have eternal life. Those who don't obey the Son will never experience eternal life, but the wrath of God remains upon them"** (John 3:36). (NLT)

NOTHING IS IMPOSSIBLE

It was a brilliant day in October 1976 in Fresno, California, when I walked out of the Fresno County Jail. I had been inside the jail to visit an inmate, not to serve time! While ministering at Valley Medical Center as a chaplain, I had met José, an inmate from the Fresno County Jail. He had become ill while in the jail and spent several days at the hospital. While talking to him I led him to faith in Christ as his personal Savior and when he was to be discharged back to the jail he asked me if I would come see him in the jail. I said, "Sure," not knowing what I was getting into.

When I walked out of the Fresno County Jail on that beautiful October day I was very depressed. This was the first time I had ever been inside a jail and the conditions gave me a great sense of depression. On that beautiful day I said to myself, "I will never go inside that jail again." Boy, was I wrong! Someone has said if you want to make God chuckle just tell him your plans. I think God must have laughed right out loud!

It was on that October day that I mentioned above that I went to see José. José was in the medical section of the jail in a room designated 2C-3. It was a small room (just José in there) with no windows and it was very depressing to see this man in such poor conditions (thankfully after the jail was remodeled in the early 1990's this room no longer existed). It was when I walked out of the jail, so depressed, that I made the remark above.

God's timing is interesting and sometimes even amusing. It wasn't more than a few days later when Chaplain Knight, who was the head chaplain at the jail, asked if I would come help him at the jail. I said, "NO," maybe not quite that loud, but I said I did not want to come work in the jail. But Chaplain Knight persisted. He said he needed help and if I could come for only two or three weeks, or even for one week, it would be of great help to him. I thought to myself, this man really needs help and I can stand anything for two or three weeks, even that jail, so I said, "OK, I will come help you for two or three weeks." Thirty-four years later I retired! Thank you, Lord, for your guidance.

Those thirty-four years is what this book is all about. It's about how God changed lives, the lives of men and women who had spent their lives in drugs, gangs and crime. In the years that I spent ministering in the jail there were hundreds who professed faith in Christ. The stories of some of those are recorded in this book. They are stories of how God works in peoples' lives and changes them and shows that "Nothing is Impossible with God."

Today, for one to become a chaplain or chaplain's volunteer at the jail you have to go through a background check. Your name is sent to Sacramento and they check you out to see if you have a criminal record, but when I started things were much simpler. Chaplain Knight wrote on the back of his business card, "Chaplain Davis works with me," and I used this to get in and out of the jail.

It worked fine for a couple of days, but then one of the clerks, who had to pop a lock on a locked door to let me out, wouldn't open the door. Instead he called a sergeant. I thought, "Wow, am I going to spend the night in jail?!"

Sargeant Brittain came and I showed him the business card. He said to the clerk, "This is Chaplain Knight's handwriting and this looks OK to me, let Chaplain Davis out." This was the beginning of a long friendship with Sergeant Brittain, one of my favorite sergeants at the jail.

After a short time I was issued an official ID card with my picture on it. The jail captain, Captain Dennis, interviewed me in his office. He asked me my age and I said, "Forty-five." He just sat there looking at me for what seemed the longest time. Finally I got embarrassed and said, "Don't you believe me?" (A lot of people thought I looked older than I really was.) He smiled and said, "Yes, I was trying to figure out the color of your hair." I said, "It used to be black, but it is pretty gray now." When I got my ID card it said, "hair color-gray/black."

My first week at the jail (in fact, my whole jail ministry) was one of the greatest times of my life. All day long the officers would bring men to the chaplains' office and I would talk with them about the Lord for an hour or more. What a blessing! Never in all my ministry (22 years as a pastor) had I had such an opportunity to share about the Lord Jesus Christ and the Word of God. Each day I would see from four to seven men. Many of these men accepted Christ as their Savior and I would see them in my office on a weekly basis for further counsel and study of the Bible. Some of their testimonies you will read later in this book.

Of course, I had never been in a jail before or around those who worked in one, so I was not familiar with "jail" language. A few days after I started working at the jail I asked an officer to bring me a certain inmate. When the officer appeared without the inmate he said, "Chaplain, he has rolled up." The only thing I could think of was that the inmate was not feeling well and had gone back to bed, rolled up in his bunk. I said, "That's OK, I will call him later this week." Actually, what the officer meant was that the inmate had left the jail. I still remember that officer looking at me and talking to me as one would to a small child as he said, "Chaplain, he rolled up. He is not here. He is gone, he is not here." That is how I learned that "rolled up" meant you had left the jail. By the way, if you ever saw an inmate leave the jail you would know why they call it "rolled up." The inmate would place all his belongings on his mattress, roll it up and put it on his shoulder, and go down to booking to be booked out. He literally "rolled up" all his belongings in his mattress.

As that first week was winding down I remembered that I had told Rev. Knight that I would help him for only two or three weeks. I was afraid that at the end of the three weeks he would let me go, so at the end of the week I went up to him and said, "Russell, I will stay as long as you want me to stay." He let me stay! It was eleven years later that Chaplain Knight was called home to glory and thirty-four years later that I would retire.

After about two months at the jail Chaplain Knight told me that he had been watching me to see if I got along well, not only with the inmates, but with jail staff as well. He told me that I had passed his scrutiny as he felt that I related well to the officers.

There were a couple of officers that at first I did seem to have a hard time relating to. One worked the security station on the third floor where our office was located so I saw a lot of him, but he always seemed rather cool towards me.

I had been working at the jail for only a short time when one day, as I came by the security station, this officer who worked the security station, and two or three other officers, were discussing the death penalty. This officer looked at me and said with a sneer, "I suppose you don't believe in the death penalty." My reply was, "I sure do," and we were instant friends—I mean from that moment on we were friends. Until he retired he was one of my best friends at the jail. Even after his retirement I would sometimes see him on the streets and he was always friendly.

There was another officer that I had a hard time being friendly with. He didn't seem to respond to me in a friendly way. But just like the other officer this relationship would change in an instant. One day as we were talking, I don't recall what he said, but my answer was, "I put my pants on one leg at a time just like anyone else," an instant change. He was always friendly after that. If he came into the dining room when I was eating he would always come and sit with me. I guess he had thought up to that point that I had thought I was better than others. Anyway, we became good friends.

He always liked a little story I told him once and he even asked me to tell it to other officers if they were eating with us. The story was this: a father was trying to teach his little son to always pray before eating, but he just couldn't seem to get the little guy to do it. The little fellow would just start right in eating. Finally, when one day the father said, "Son, we need to pray before we eat," the little guy said, "Don't have to—Mom's a good cook!"

For most of the first two years that I worked at the jail much of my time was spent in counseling inmates one-on-one. In the next chapter I will tell you about some of those with whom I counseled, but first let me tell about one of the highlights of that first year at the jail. It was when I met the last surviving member of the Bonnie and Clyde gang.

Chaplain Knight and I had gone to Portland, Oregon, for a chaplains' conference. One of those who had a booth at the conference was Chaplain Ray of International Prison Ministries. Chaplain Ray was one of the first to start a ministry that focused on reaching those incarcerated in our prisons and jails. Several others have started ministries since, such as Chuck Colson's "Prison Fellowship" and Bill Glass with his "Weekend of Champions," but Chaplain Ray was the first and was looked upon as the Father of Prison Ministries. Later, Chaplain Ray would visit our jail in Fresno.

Though it was great to meet Chaplain Ray, it was the

man with him who intrigued me the most, Floyd Hamilton. We had a magazine which we handed out in the jail with Floyd's story in it. The title of the story was, "The Last of the Bonnie and Clyde Gang." Floyd was the driver of the get-away car for the Barrow gang and participated in many crimes with Bonnie and Clyde. His brother, Raymond, was also a member of the gang. Since I had read his story it was a special privilege to talk with him. I wish now that I had gotten his autograph.

When I met Floyd he was almost seventy years old. He had been released from Alcatraz 20 years earlier in 1956. He was of medium build and he was very soft-spoken. It was hard to realize that at one time he was "public enemy number one" and that he had spent the longest time in Alcatraz of any other inmate, 25 years and 1 month.

Floyd had also written a book, "Public Enemy Number One," which we distributed to our inmates. There are three things that I especially remember from that book.

Floyd relates a story of how he and his partner robbed a bank and sped out of town in their get-away car. They knew the police would soon be on the chase after them so they stopped and quickly changed license plates. As they got back in their car they could hear the police sirens coming towards them. They turned around and headed back towards the oncoming police cars. It was just getting dark and he said as they met each police car the officers would throw their spotlight onto their license plate and keep going. Soon they met the last car and then headed out of town in the opposite direction and made their escape!

Also, he tells of the time that he and three others tried to escape from Alcatraz. They had built a flotation device to help in their escape, but somehow they left it behind in the prison when they made their break. Two of his companions were killed as they were escaping and the other was recaptured in the bay shortly afterwards.

Floyd managed to get into a cave on the side of the island. He said it was filled with a lot of old tires and when the officers entered the cave to search for him he was able to elude capture by hiding among those tires. He was there for two days, wet, cold and hungry. He finally realized he could never escape without that flotation device so he broke back into the prison to retrieve it. He said as he got back into the prison it was so warm and he was so cold that he sat down to rest for a minute and fell asleep. When he awoke a guard was standing over him with a gun pointed at him and he was taken back to his cell. Thus, none of the four made good on their escape attempt.

The escape attempt took place in 1943 and even though Floyd had this attempted escape on his record he was finally paroled in 1956. As he was leaving the prison a guard said to him, "Hamilton, where are you going?" and Floyd said, "I am going home." The officer laughed and said, "This is your home, Hamilton." But Floyd told him that he had found the Lord Jesus as his Master and that he would stay out. Floyd was now a changed man, changed by the grace and power of God, and he was never again imprisoned.

Once Floyd was out of prison he couldn't wait to go to a restaurant and have a chicken dinner. So he did. In prison they ate with real silverware, not the plastic knives and forks we gave the inmates at the jail. After each meal in the prison they had to take their silverware up to a guard so the officer would know they were not taking it back to their cell to use as a weapon. Floyd enjoyed his chicken dinner and after he had finished eating he picked up his silverware and took it over and gave it to the cashier!

In the following pages of this book you will read the stories of some of the men and women that it was my privilege to lead to Christ and/or to disciple in the Christian faith at the Fresno County Jail in Fresno, California. Some of these will be sharing their testimonies. These testimonies are shared, not to exalt the individual, but to show that we have a Great God Who can change anyone. No matter how hopeless you may think your life is, GOD CAN CHANGE YOU, for the Bible–the Book of Truth–says, **"For nothing is impossible with God"** (Luke 1:37). (NLT, KJV)

2

TELL ME ABOUT YOURSELF

As I said, most of what I did for the first two years in the jail was counsel inmates in the chaplains' office. The jail had four stories and the chaplains' office was on the third floor. I would have a list of men who wanted to talk to me in private. I would either phone the floor where the inmate was housed and ask for him to be sent down, or I would go up to the floor and ask for him. After I had returned to my office, an officer would bring the inmate to me and we would have an hour or more to talk.

The chaplains' office was just big enough to have a desk, my chair, and a chair for the inmate. Many of these men I still remember and some of them are still in touch with me today. We had a very relaxed atmosphere. I even let them smoke if they wished until the jail put a ban on smoking in the jail. We would share the Word of God together, cry together, and laugh together. When a new man came in, I would say to him, "Tell me about yourself," and what stories I would hear. How I wish now that I had kept the notes I made then, but a number of years ago I thought that I would no longer need them so I disposed of them. Big mistake.

Chaplain Knight would give me names of men who wished to talk to me and I would put them on my list. We also had inmate request slips which the inmates had in their cells and they would send me a request and ask to come talk with me. The inmates called these request slips "kites." I didn't know that they called them that and I still recall the first time an inmate told me, "Chaplain, I will fly you a kite." I didn't have a clue what he meant! I thought, "Man, you are locked up and it isn't even windy outside; how can you fly me a kite?" Of course, all he was saying was, "I will send you a request slip."

One day an inmate in 4C on the fourth floor of the jail came up to the bars and said, "Chaplain, I would like to come down to your office and talk with you." I said to him, "Fine, but unless this is an emergency it will be three or four days before I can see you." He replied, "That's OK, Chaplain. I am not going anywhere!"

Even though it has now been almost 40 years, I still remember the very first inmate who came to talk to me. His name was Mike and he made a profession of faith in Christ. It would be great to have Mike's testimony in this book as a strong Christian, but such was not the case. Mike was in and out of jail and prison for the next 20 years or more. The last time I talked to him was when he called to tell me his brother had died in prison. His brother and I had a long relationship and later on I will tell you about him. There will also be a chapter on some of those who, like Mike, made professions of faith but just couldn't seem to make it in society. Hopefully, Mike has found out how to be a success with the Lord Jesus as his Savior.

Mike, if you ever read this, get in touch. I would love to hear from you.

During those first couple of years I interviewed many inmates. As I said, I would keep a record of each inmate and the interview in a notebook. If I were seeing the inmate on a regular basis, before he would come to see me I would read over what we had discussed the previous week. When we started our discussion I was thus able to recall what we had talked about before. Some of the men were really impressed at my great memory! I never did tell my secret.

Roy was from Canada. He and his partner came to California with an ingenious scheme. They bought traveler's checks of 100 Deutsche Marks which cost them $22 each. They would then go into small towns on the weekend, when the banks were closed, and cash these in the stores as 100 dollar traveler's checks. Obviously they were making a profit of $78 on each traveler's check. It worked fine until they got caught. When they were arrested in a small town just east of Fresno, Roy had over $5000 in cash in his possession.

The first time Roy came to see me he told me how his grandmother was a good Christian lady. This gave me the opportunity to discuss what the Bible says about how to become a Christian and how a Christian should live.

As we finished our interview, and just before we left to take Roy back down to the second floor where he was housed, he made two requests. The first was that he would like to phone his wife in Canada. The jail didn't have phones in the cells then as they do now for the inmates to use. However, I could sometimes get a call for an inmate, so when I took Roy back down on the second floor I asked the officer at the security station if he could make a collect call to his wife in Canada. No problem, so I left him at the security station talking to his wife while I went back to see about his second request.

His second request was that a man be moved out of his tank. Roy had said there was an inmate in his tank named Mr. M. and that if he were not moved out there was going to be a fight. Now it so happened that the classification office (where it was decided where inmates were housed) was right outside Roy's tank and Jimmy, the assistant classification officer, was there. I said, "Jimmy, I just had Roy up in my office and he told me that if Mr. M..." Before I could finish, Jimmy said, "Yes, Chaplain, we know and I am rolling him out right now." I said to Jimmy, "Boy, you are really on the ball," and I went back to my office on the third floor.

When Roy finished his phone call, he met Mr. M. and an officer in the hall as Mr. M. was being moved to another tank. The next time Roy saw me he didn't say "hello" or "how are you," he just blurted out, "Man, you really get things done around here!" I never did tell him that Jimmy was rolling Mr. M. up before I ever talked to him!

Roy was a very likeable fellow and we became friends. Later, after he had done his time in jail, his wife came from Canada to pick him up. Roy asked me if I would perform a service for them where they could renew their marriage vows. This I was glad to do and we went out to a park in Fresno and had a brief ceremony.

Henry came to my office for Bible study and counseling each week. One week he said, "Chaplain, before I leave I have a prayer request to share with you." After we had finished talking, I said, "What is your prayer request?" Now let me explain something. In those days the jail did their own food service for the inmates. Most of the meals were refried beans, rice, etc., but once a week they served real chicken. I mean it was good stuff and the inmates looked forward to it. However, they never served chicken on the same day each week. Why? I don't know. Maybe they wanted to keep the inmates looking forward to having chicken. Anyway, when I asked Henry what his request was, he said, "Chaplain, the Lord has laid on my heart to fast one day next week. Please pray I don't pick the day they serve chicken!"

Another incident happened when I was counseling a man who was a union organizer. He was in jail for destroying several vehicles of a company that the union was striking. After several sessions he seemed desirous of committing his life to Christ. However, he had a question. He asked me if he accepted Christ as his Lord and Savior could he still destroy vehicles if the union was on strike. I said, "No, you would have to obey the law." He looked at me for a few moments and said, "I want a second opinion!" To my knowledge, he never did make a decision to follow Christ.

One day as I was counseling an inmate he began to talk about his brother. Finally, I said to him, "You mean you and your brother look alike?" He said, "We sure do. If my brother were standing in that door (and he pointed to the door of our office) you couldn't tell us apart." "Are you and your brother twins?" I asked. He replied, "We sure are, born eleven months apart!"

Ted came to my office one day and the first thing he said to me was, "Chaplain, I am the Father, the Son and the Holy Ghost." After we had talked for a while Ted said, "Chaplain, l am not the Father, am I?" I said, "No, Ted, you are not." Soon he said, "Chaplain, I am not the Son either, am I?" I said, "No, Ted, you are not." Shortly after that we had prayer and Ted left.

The next day I had to go down to booking and I had to walk right past our three safety cells. A safety cell was a rubber-padded room where an inmate was put for his own protection if he were mentally unstable. There was just a small iron grate that the inmate could look out of or the officers could look in to check his condition. What I didn't know was that Ted had freaked out the night before and he was in one of the safety cells. As I walked by the cells I heard this plaintive voice out of the blue say, "Chaplain, I am not the Holy Ghost either, am I?"

One time a man who had murdered his wife wanted to come to see me. I set up an appointment. Now the last few men that I had counseled who were in for killing their spouses had all told me how much they had loved their wives. As I waited for this man I said, "Lord, don't let him tell me how much he loved his wife." As he came into my office and sat down, he burst into tears and said, "I loved her so!" I wanted to say, "I hope you don't love me!"

Jim was out of the protective custody tank (called PC for

short), and he was not the brightest bulb on the Christmas tree. After we had talked for quite a while, I said, "Jim, you have to go back to your tank," and he began to cry. He was shedding buckets of tears and then he began to slobber and then his nose began to run with a lot of gook. Then he wanted to put his head on my shoulder!

As I said, Jim was PC, which meant he couldn't be mixed with other inmates. After our interview I had to escort him down the hall to the security station and have an officer take him back to his cell. When I finally got Jim calmed down (by the way, I didn't let him put his head on my shoulder!), we left the office. I locked the door and we started for the security station. We got about halfway down the hall when here came a whole bunch of inmates going back to their tank from the exercise yard on the roof. I tried to get Jim back into my office, but I was so nervous that I couldn't get the key to work. Jim was milling around among the inmates and I was perspiring profusely. Finally, I got the door open and Jim safely inside.

When I thought all was clear we started back down to the security station and here came about six more inmates! I got Jim off to one side and we edged by them. I don't think I would have been much protection for Jim! When we got to the security station the security officer said, "Chaplain, you sure picked a bad time to bring this man back. There were about six inmates in that group who would have liked to beat the stuffing out of him!" I don't remember what I said to the officer, but it was something like, "Man, you don't know how hard I tried!" But I do know that I was thankful for God's protection.

Brownie was another inmate with whom I counseled in those early days at the jail. He was involved in gangs and later his estranged wife and her boyfriend were murdered execution-style by a rival gang, but that was sometime after Brownie had left for prison. Brownie could not come to her funeral so he asked if I would go in his place. I did, and I still remember the service which was held at St. John's Catholic Church in Fresno.

As I said, it was October when I started working at the jail and when Christmas came, Brownie asked if I would go see his mother. She lived fairly close to where I lived, though he didn't know that, and I told him I would go see her for him.

When I got to his mother's place that night, I found his father drunk and barely able to sit in his chair. There was also a brother there, a rather husky, mean-looking character. I had a nice visit with his mother and when it came time for me to leave, she asked me to pray. Before I could pray, big, mean-looking brother said, "We don't want any prayer in this house." My thought was, "Hey, whatever you say, big guy." But I will never forget that little (when I say "little" I mean "little"—she probably didn't weigh 90 pounds!) mother's statement. She pointed to the floor and said, "This is my house and if I say we can pray, we will pray." I prayed.

As I left the house and was walking across the yard (quite a large yard) to my car I heard footsteps and glanced back and here came big, old mean-looking brother! I quickened my steps and got to the car before he could get too close. He came up to the window and apologized for what he had said. Later, he was arrested and spent some time in jail and he and I became friends. In fact, he was arrested several times and each time he came to jail he would send out a "kite" and ask me to come see him.

Brownie trusted Christ as his Savior before he went to prison. Upon his release he returned to Fresno and the last I heard of him he was still walking with Christ.

"Twenty-two, twenty-two, sixty-six, twenty-two, twenty-two." These were the first words out of the mouth of Bobby Ray as he sat down in a chair in my office. I didn't have a clue what he was talking about. Then he told me. These were the number of verses in each of the five chapters of the Book of Lamentations in the Bible.

Bobby Ray was one of the more notorious inmates in our jail. He had been arrested for multiple killings, one of them a contract killing. He was eventually sentenced to Death Row at San Quentin Prison. While on Death Row I heard that he was charged with killing another inmate. He spent many years on Death Row before dying of natural causes in 2007 at the age of 58.

Speaking of Death Row, when I started work at the jail in 1976 there were 34 inmates on death row, now there are over 700. One of the last to be executed was Clarence, who came through our facility before I started working at the jail. Later, his son, who was an accomplice of Bobby Ray, did five years in our jail while waiting for trial.

Bobby Ray's girlfriend had also been his accomplice in the murders he had committed. She held a gun on the four people Bobby Ray murdered with a single barrel shotgun. While she was in jail, she counseled with my wife, Myrna. To my knowledge she is still in prison.

Craig came to faith in Christ in the first few years of my ministry at the jail. His coming to faith in Christ was different and to me interesting as we see how God works. As we often say, "You can't put God in a box." Craig was confined on the fourth floor in tank 4F. He was lying on his bunk and one of our volunteers was at the bars witnessing to another inmate. Craig listened as the way of salvation was explained and Craig asked Christ into his life. I don't know about the other inmate and I am sure that our volunteer never knew of the fruit that his witness had borne in Craig's life.

Later Craig was transferred to the branch jail, some 20 miles west of Fresno, where he served his time. Upon his release he became active in a local church and eventually he returned to the branch jail as the chaplain.

While he was serving as chaplain at the branch jail, he and I were asked to speak to a local group that was interested in jail ministry. I did not realize it at the time, but I said something that upset Craig. About a year after the meeting he came to me and told me what I had said and how it had made him mad, but now he realized that what I said was right and that his attitude was wrong. What had I said? I had quoted a missionary named Don Hillis who said, "Evangelism without discipleship is not evangelism." Craig had thought if he could just lead people in the "sinner's prayer" he had done what God wanted, but now he saw that we must follow up and disciple those who put their faith in Christ.

Craig served at the branch jail for about two years and then he accepted a call from a church in the state of Oregon to come and be their pastor.

Some of those who I counseled would contact me after they left jail. One man said he wrote me, but he didn't have my office address so he wrote me at the jail address. His letter was sent back to him marked, "Not in custody!" Through the years I corresponded with many inmates as they served time in prison.

In the jail I ministered to people from all over the world, even the Mid-East and Russia. Most of the inmates had an average education, but there were two that I ministered to who were well-educated. One was a psychologist and the other had a PhD and said he was a former professor at Purdue University. While still incarcerated this latter one wrote me the following letter after he and I had had a counseling session:

Dear Rev. Davis, I want to take this opportunity to thank you for helping me turn my mind and heart closer to God through Jesus Christ. I have always led a "cultural Christian" life but I have not (obviously) fully accepted Jesus Christ as my Lord and Savior...You, with God's will, have helped me find the true meaning of why Christ died for me and how this relates to how I live my life here on earth...For this I am truly grateful. In addition to your encouragement the books by Dr. James Gill helped me greatly. I started on his book titled, LOVE; here I came to grips with the selfishness that characterized my entire adult life...I then read Dr. Gill's book IMAGINATIONS – what a powerful book! It is here that I truly turned my mind and heart closer to God...I unconditionally accepted Jesus Christ as my Lord and Savior and his ways as my lifestyle...."

We would occasionally have contact with an inmate's family. Though I never met Steven's parents, I share a letter which they wrote me. This is taken from our Summer 2006 newsletter:

Dear Mr. Davis, We received a call last night from Steven asking us to E-mail you and THANK YOU for the Bible you sent him. He is so happy that it is a red letter edition which he likes....We, his parents, cannot thank you enough for the work you are doing. Steven was very bitter towards us and sent us an 8-page letter telling us so. We wondered what changed his attitude and now we find out you were there having some Bible study with him and his cell mates. We were praying daily for the Lord to send someone to help him and now he tells of the good Bible study he had. Our prayer is that the Lord will use him in the future to lead a Bible study or be a real light for the Lord in prison. That is the only reason we can see for the Lord to make **"all things work together for good."**

As I look back on this part of my ministry, I realize that not only was it a great pleasure to me, but lasting fruit for God came forth from these counseling sessions and Bible studies: three are now ordained ministers, two became Area Directors for Prison Fellowship, and another worked with Prison Fellowship's "Network for Life." Several, such as Barry, Rocky, Rosemary, Rosie, Vickie, Richard, David and others became jail volunteers and worked with us at the Fresno County Jail.

One of the women to whom Chaplain Nancy Dixon ministered in the jail even went back, after her conversion to

Christ and release from prison, to the very prison where she had served time, and worked as a member of the prison staff.

As we see how God brought each of these, and many others, to Himself as God's Word was shared through personal counseling, chapel services, and personal Bible studies, we are reminded that the Bible–the Book of Truth–says: **"The rain and snow come down from the heavens and stay on the ground to water the earth. They cause the grain to grow, producing seed for the farmer and bread for the hungry. It is the same with My Word. I send it out, and it always produces fruit. It will accomplish all I want it to, and it will prosper everywhere I send it"** (Isaiah 55:10-11). (NLT)

3

ON THE FLOOR

After I had been in the jail and counseling for a while, I began to go out on the floor with Chaplain Knight and talk to the men in their cells. This, too, I greatly enjoyed, along with the one-on-one counseling which I continued to do.

We did not go inside the housing units as we did later in the new jail, but we would go down the hall and talk to the men who would come up to the bars to talk to us. To get to the men in some of the tanks on the third floor, the officers would remotely open a door for us and we would step into a cage and talk to those who came up to the bars.

Each of the tanks in our old jail had different classifications (as is still true today). There were three basic classifications, minimum, medium and maximum. Inmates with different classification were never mixed with each other. Each tank had a day room and then all around the edge of the day room were the cells where the inmates slept. This cell was their "home." Each cell would usually hold four to six men. During the day the men would sit at tables in the day room and play cards, tell "war stories," etc. At night they were all put in their cells. When it came time to go to their cells for the night, usually at 9:00 PM, an officer would call over the intercom, "RACK UP!" This meant leave the day room and go to your cell. One of the sergeants told me once that instead of telling his kids to go to bed at night he would say, "Rack up," and they knew what he meant.

Not only were there different classifications but various inmates were dressed differently so that their status could be easily and quickly determined. Most inmates now wear red jumpsuits, but when I first started to work at the jail most of the inmates wore jeans with a red sweatshirt. Men who were "high power" (those considered more dangerous) wore yellow sweatshirts. Trustees were dressed in blue. A trustee was an inmate who had been convicted and was serving local time. These trustees were used not only inside the jail but some worked on the grounds outside the jail. An officer said to me one day, "I don't know why they call them 'trustees,' we know they are criminals."

An officer told me an amusing story about an inmate who was being released and had no clothing to wear home. After some discussion it was decided to let him wear his jeans and red sweatshirt home. Shortly after his release here came a deputy sheriff with this man in his patrol car. The deputy was bringing back this escapee! He explained how he had caught this man several blocks from the jail and arrested him for an attempted escape from the jail. The officers present started laughing and told him that the inmate had been released and they had allowed him to wear the jail clothing home. The deputy said, "Yeah, he kept telling me that, but I didn't believe him."

Besides the above three normal classifications there were special classifications such as "protective custody" (PC) and "high power," as I mentioned previously. The men in "PC" were housed in 3C. These were inmates who had committed crimes against children, or were informers (snitches), gang dropouts, etc. If they were mixed with regular inmates there was a good chance they would be beaten up or worse. The "Jim" I talked about in chapter two was out of this tank. Inmates in this tank could not mingle in the dayroom but were locked in their cells 24/7. These cells were about 5' by 9' with four bunks and usually there were four men in the cell. One cell at a time was let out for showers, etc. There was also a tank trustee who would take coffee and hot water to those in their cells. A coffee pot was always in each tank. If the tank was on discipline for some reason, the coffee pot was usually removed.

The longest sentence a person could receive to do jail time was one year, and out of this year four months were deducted for "good time." Sometimes an inmate would receive two one-year sentences. Sentences were usually run concurrent, that is, if one was given two one-year sentences in jail, they would be run together and he would actually do only eight months in jail. Sometimes, though, they would be run consecutive. They would have to do one of the one-year sentences, then they would do the additional year so they actually spent 16 months in jail.

An inmate told me one time that he had received two one-year sentences and they had run them "bow-legged" on him. He had to explain to me that he meant they had run them consecutive. One inmate that I knew received two one-year sentences and they were run "bow-legged" on him. He spent 16 months cooped up in one of those 5' by 9' cells in "protective custody" in 3C.

Men who were classified as "high power" were the hardened criminals, those who were incorrigible and were a threat to other inmates and even to our officers. Whenever they were taken anywhere (such as to court, etc.), they were shackled both hands and feet and two officers had to be with them. Barry, whom I will tell about later, was "high power." Barry was a big guy, six foot three and about 250 pounds. He once had an altercation with one of our officers so he was always handled with extreme care.

After Barry became a Christian he used to come into the jail and speak to the men in chapel services. One night he was late so I went upstairs without him. Right after our service started here came a sergeant escorting Barry to the service. I thought to myself, "Sergeant, a few years ago you would have had Barry shackled hand and foot and another officer would have been with you." God changes people.

Incidentally, speaking of "high power" and being handcuffed, whenever a parole officer came to take an inmate to the outside they always handcuffed him to prevent his trying to run away. Once two parole officers came to take a young, 18-year-old inmate down to the parole office. This young man had a broken arm and had his arm in a sling. There was no way they could handcuff him, but they agreed that with his arm in a sling there was no way he could outrun both of them and escape, but he did!

The men in "high power" were housed in 3B in our old jail. They were locked down, that is, they were confined to their cells. These cells were identical to those in 3C and there were usually four men in each cell. In the other tanks the inmates would mingle in the day room, but not in "high power." These "high power" inmates would even fight among themselves if mixed together. As I said there was a coffee pot and hot water out in the day room and the jail would pick one man who they felt they could trust to be the "trustee" for the tank. He would take coffee and hot water to those locked in their cells. Whenever we went into 3B the "trustee" was always locked in his cell. He wasn't that trusty!

As we would go into 3B and talk with the men and give out Bibles and literature, we were always extra careful as we ministered to them. We never put our hands through the bars to shake hands (this was true of any tank as one could easily get his arm broken by doing this). We were alert to what was going on in the cell that we were ministering to, and even those close by.

In the 34 years that I worked at the jail, I never had a bad incident, thanks to the watch-care of our Great God.

Only once did I feel uneasy when I had an inmate coming to counsel with me. That was when Frank wanted to come see me and I knew he was upset with me.

Frank was unstable and could be dangerous, or so Chaplain Knight thought. He had been counseling with me for several weeks and one week he asked if I would visit his wife. I told him, "OK," so Myrna and I went to see her. However, I found out that he didn't really want me to see his wife, he just wanted me to find out where she was living, as she had moved, and he wanted to get her address from me. Of course, I refused to give it to him. This made him mad and he tried various ways to get me to give it to him, but I refused.

When he wanted to come see me one afternoon, I took our telephone and put it in our storage room lest he try to strangle me with the cord. I reasoned that without the cord, if he tried anything, I could hold him off until an officer could come to my help. Nothing happened and my precautions were not necessary.

Once Chaplain Lile noticed one of the volunteers standing too close to the bars as he talked with an inmate. Another inmate was down on the floor and about to reach through the bars and grab this volunteer's ankle and pull him off his feet. Chaplain Lile alerted the volunteer and warned him to be more careful.

As I said earlier, for some of the tanks we could walk right up to the bars and talk with interested inmates; other tanks had a "cage" and an officer would open these remotely for us from the security station. But for a couple of tanks on the second and third floors and for the dormitories on the first floor the jail issued the chaplains a key where we could unlock the door ourselves and minister to the inmates. This key would not open the actual tank where the inmates were, but only let us into a long corridor where we could talk to the inmates.

One of these tanks was 3F. Once one stepped through the locked door there was this long corridor with four cells along the side. Each of these cells housed six men. The doors were always locked to these tanks so it was perfectly safe to walk down the corridor and talk with the men.

Once when I was ministering in 3F and went down the row of cells, talking with various men, I came to tank three and found the door into the tank was wide open. As discreetly as I could I exited 3F and went up to the security station and told them the door was open and an officer was quickly dispatched to close it.

Right next to 3F was 3E and this was the same, we unlocked a door into a long corridor. However, in 3E there were just two tanks with 12 men to a tank. If we or one of our volunteers were ministering in these tanks and an officer needed to pull a man out for a visit, etc., the officer would ask us to step out into the main hall while the inmate was being pulled. I always told our volunteers, "If an officer asks you to step out, step out immediately, even if you are half-way through a prayer, step out."

In the early days when I worked at the jail the women were housed on the first floor. The men on the second, third and fourth floors would talk to them on the "toilet telephone." They would get all of the water out of the line and holler down the toilet. If the lady they were calling had her "toilet phone" on, they would converse with each other. The first time I saw this happen, this guy was kneeling over his toilet and I thought he was sick until he started hollering, then I knew he was just making a "phone" call.

In September of 1988 the local newspaper, the Fresno Bee, ran an article on our work in the jail and they had a picture of me standing in 3E talking to the inmates. Faces of the inmates could not be shown but the photographer had Ernie, one of the inmates, stick his arm through the bars so they could take a picture of his tattoos. In the article the paper reports Ernie as saying, "When I've got problems, I ask for Chaplain Davis and he talks to me about it, and he helps me pray."

Ernie had a brother, David, who was on death row in San

Quentin. David was another with whom I worked in the jail, and after he was sent to San Quentin, I visited him there on death row. He and I also corresponded for many years until my retirement in 2010.

As I went out on the floors, I carried with me two briefcases full of Bibles, New Testaments and Christian literature. Men and women who would never take time to read on the streets would read while incarcerated, so we handed out lots of literature.

When our new jail opened, we would actually go inside the pods (housing units) and talk to the men. Once I had my briefcase setting on the floor while I talked to several inmates. One inmate started to go through my briefcase and I said, "Please, don't go through my briefcase." His reply, "Do you think you can stop me?" My reply, "No." However, he stopped going through my briefcase. I was glad he did as the other inmates would probably have stopped him when they realized I didn't want him to do this. I am glad they didn't have to stop him, as this would have created an incident where the officers would probably have had to intervene, and this I did not want to happen.

One of the most popular pieces of literature we gave out was the magazine published by Chaplain Ray. Not only was Floyd Hamilton's story in it, but it had the story of Clyde Thompson, the "meanest man in Texas." In 1928, when he was only 17, he was found guilty of murder and sentenced to die in the electric chair. He was sent to death row at Huntsville Prison. He was only seven hours away from being executed when the Governor commuted his sentence to life in prison.

Thompson was so incorrigible in the first years of his imprisonment that prison officials gave him the moniker, "meanest man in Texas." Even the chaplain said that Clyde did not have a soul.

While doing time in prison, Clyde became so incorrigible that he was put into solitary confinement (the "hole") for five years. While in the "hole" he wanted something to read. He knew the only thing that the prison would allow him to have was a Bible. He asked for a Bible and it was given to him. His idea was to go through the Bible and show all the contradictions and errors and to prove that the Bible wasn't true. But the Bible is God's Word, and through his reading, the Holy Spirit brought him under conviction and he repented of his sins and received the Lord Jesus Christ as his Savior. In the Lord Jesus, the Bible, and the Holy Spirit, the "meanest man in Texas" had met his match.

Clyde's life was so changed that even while he was in the "hole" the officers would let him out to talk to other prisoners about the Lord. Thompson was eventually paroled after serving almost 30 years in prison. Some years after his release he became chaplain at the Lubbock County Jail in Lubbock, Texas. He served there faithfully until the Lord called him home. In the Apostle Paul, God saved the "chief of sinners" (I Timothy 1:15), and in Clyde Thompson, God saved the "meanest" of sinners. In Christ there is hope for anybody.

Besides Chaplain Ray's magazine we handed out many other books written by former drug addicts and ex-cons. One of the most popular was Jerry Graham's story, "Where Flies Don't Land." Jerry was a hardcore addict; he once took 13 black beauties, a powerful drug in pill form. This should have killed him, but it didn't. Jerry was almost put away as a habitual criminal, but he gave his life to Christ and eventually was set free. Jerry came into our jail several times with the Bill Glass "Weekend of Champions."

Jerry Graham also worked with Chaplain Ray and it was one of the times Myrna and I went out with Chaplain Ray that we met Jerry. Myrna and I were in a restaurant when he came in. I recognized him and we went over and introduced ourselves. It was interesting to talk to a man who I had read about many times. Jerry was just a great guy and very easy to get to know.

While we were out on the floor handing out Bibles and

literature we would also give out the GOSPEL ECHOES BIBLE STUDIES (which I will tell you about in a later chapter) and collect the test sheets that the inmates had to complete when they finished the Bible study. When an inmate completed four lessons, he got a Bible with his name on it. Then for the next four lessons he would get a certificate to show that he had done the lessons. One time I took a certificate to an inmate. He was a man about 40 years of age and, as I gave him his certificate, tears came to his eyes and he said, "Chaplain, this is the first time I have ever earned anything on my own."

Just writing about this brings to my mind the many times that I stood at those bars and talked to men about their relationship to Christ, or discussed some Bible passage or gave a word of encouragement and had a prayer with them. It was a ministry I deeply enjoyed and I am sure God did a real work in many lives as we shared the Word of God with them.

Robert – *Sentenced to Life*

In the following chapter you will read Robert's testimony. Robert was sentenced to life in prison under California's Three Strikes law. The law said that if you were convicted of three felonies you could be sent to prison for 25 years to life. The felonies were supposed to have violence in them, but this was not always followed in the sentencing of an individual. Such was the case with Robert.

Robert was arrested in 1995 and sentenced in 1996 under the Three Strikes law. His crime: he had taken his girlfriend's purse and wouldn't give it back so she called the police. By the time the police arrived he had returned the purse and all was well. However, since Robert was on parole, he was arrested and charged with a misdemeanor and his third strike. There had been violence in his first two crimes (both felonies), but not this one.

Robert was sent to Wasco State Prison as a parole violator

and after a few months was returned to Fresno County Jail to await his trial. As you will see from his testimony, while at Wasco he gave his life to Christ and when he returned to Fresno, I began to disciple him. He began to study the Bible through our Gospel Echoes Bible studies and I could see real growth in his life.

Robert was in a Security Housing Unit (SHU). These men were not allowed to come to our chapel services because all had a violent past. Though Robert was in a SHU unit he was allowed to come to the chapel services and he came faithfully. By the time Robert went for sentencing he had become strong in Christ and had committed all into the hands of the Lord Jesus Christ.

An interesting side note to Robert's story is that his sister, Vickie, had been in our jail just a few years previous to Robert's being there. Vickie had given her life to Christ and my wife, Myrna, counseled with Vickie over the time that she was incarcerated. This was over 30 years ago and Vickie is still walking with Christ and is going into the jail as a chaplains' volunteer.

Someone has said, "Sin will take you farther than you want to go, keep you longer than you want to stay, and make you pay more than you want to pay." But Jesus, in the Bible–the Book of Truth–says: **"The thief's purpose is to steal and kill and destroy. My purpose is to give life in all its fullness"** (Saint John 10:10). (NLT)

4

THREE STRIKES

MY TESTIMONY
by Robert Valdez

On the afternoon of June 25, 1995, I was alone in my cell at Wasco State Prison Reception Center (called "fish row" by the inmates because what goes on becomes common knowledge throughout the prison) doing a parole violation out of Fresno County. As I looked out the small window of my cell I wasn't feeling like my usual self. There was a tug on my heart that seemed to be pulling harder and harder.

I was caught up in a life-style of drug addiction, crime and violence that eventually led me into a gang. To me it was a dream come true, hanging out with the fellas that were well-known, getting loaded smoking yesca (marijuana), and drinking every day.

Wherever I went my reputation preceded me—in the courthouse, in prison and on the streets. It was known that I never ran from a fight—I ran to them! Throughout my hometown in Fresno, California, I was notorious and eventually the notoriety followed me to prison.

As I write this testimony I give all glory to God. He had a plan. This tug on my heart finally brought me to my knees beside my bunk, crying out to the Lord, "Help me, I need you." I never cried before, not even at my Mother's funeral.

While crying and asking for forgiveness I started feeling sort of a "high." A heavy burden was gone. I did not know I was praying. I was still trapped in the cell and had not realized that I was already free on the inside. All of a sudden this spiritual hunger hit me. I wanted a Bible. It took me about three days to get one on "fish row" but I did get one.

A violation for petty theft had landed me back behind bars and after going to the Morrissey Board I was headed to Tehachapi State Prison to serve my 11 month violation. As I was waiting for the chain (men were shackled to a chain when being transported, hence, "waiting for the chain" meant one was waiting to be transported), I'm called to "roll-up" and catch the "gray goose" (Sheriff's bus) back to Fresno County. I thought, "Okay, I'll be paroling from the county jail."

When I got to Fresno I immediately made plans to see Chaplain Davis to find out if my whole experience of conversion was a legitimate one. I wanted to know if I was truly saved or just going through the motions. I put my request in from the infirmary. I was single-celled because I had an I.V. in my arm for an infection on my chest. Chaplain Davis came to see me and brought me a Bible. I explained to him the weeping and crying out to the Lord on my knees in the cell at Wasco Reception Center. He was very surprised as he prayed with me and led me down the Romans Road of Salvation in the Book of Romans (see Appendix A, pg. 165). He told me to read my Bible and gave me some correspondence Bible studies from Emmaus.

Throughout my twenty-five years of going in and out of the Fresno County jail I never in my life did time like this. When I was incarcerated I had heard the Gospel message through Rev. Knight, Chaplain Davis and Chaplain Lile. Message after message were preached by these holy men of God. But I was only going to the church service in the county jail to pick-up (score), pass a kite, or see the homeboys from other tanks, 3A, 3D and 3F in the old county jail in Fresno.

- 32 -

The chapel service was always on the second floor. It was also a way of getting out of the tank in which one was locked up to take care of business.

Little did I know that the Word of God never comes back void. **"So shall my Word be that goes out from my mouth; it shall not return to me empty but it shall accomplish that which I purpose and shall succeed in the thing for which I sent it"** (Isaiah 55:11). (NRSV) *Now I know that the Word of God is true.*

After I was well I was taken out of the infirmary and housed on the fifth floor of the Main Jail in a secure housing unit. I faithfully attended Chaplain Davis's Life Changing Class for eight months. No inmate is supposed to come out of the pod I was in to attend Bible studies or church services, but I was permitted to go to the class. To God be the glory, He opened the doors for me! Chaplain Davis said this had never happened before in the new county jail (fifth floor).

I thank God for Chaplain Davis and his labor of love and many years serving as a chaplain and never giving up. To this day I correspond with him via mail and phone calls to speak and share with him how the Lord is using me. I pray for him daily. He has encouraged me and always said that I can overcome the impossible (Luke 1:37).

Through faith in God and applying His Word in my life I am a new man (II Corinthians 5:17). I've been born again and saved by grace alone through faith alone (Ephesians 2:8, 9).

Chaplain Davis has taught me the essential core teaching of Christianity. This teaching is that God provided redemption for our sins by Jesus' atoning work on the cross, the Deity of Christ, the Virgin Birth and Incarnation of Jesus Christ. This teaching is how to be approved by God by studying His Word (II Timothy 2:15). To this day he is my spiritual father, mentor and best friend and has taught me how to be a leader as a man of God. Through the years he has led by example. He has touched my heart and has taught me to add value to all men by serving them in life (Luke 21:19). In addition to his spiritual guidance he has supplied me with commentaries, Bible handbooks and advice through godly counsel, not only for myself but to share with and minister to others.

By now my eleven months were up and I am still in the county jail wondering why I have not been called to be released on parole. So I decided to call my sister, Mary, to find out if I'll be getting out soon. She tells me that they lost my file.

The next morning they call me for court and then when I get there they send me back to the tank saying they made a mistake. I tell my sister again to call the courthouse to see if I am going to be released. They told her, "No, he is facing a three-strike case." Twenty-five years to life for petty theft!

After hearing this bad news I understood the blow for which God had prepared me. The DA refiled and hit me with three-strikes. Bruce Hood, associate chaplain from the Fresno County Jail, was at my hearing trying to get me to a Christian program. A representative from another rehabilitation program, the Potter's Wheel, was also there and making a plea on my behalf, but to no avail.

As the judge pronounced, "I sentence you to 25 years to life," my heart fell and all the members of my family were shattered. I was determined to let everyone know why Jesus Christ called me out of darkness on a mission from God into His marvelous light. So I began to pray and ask the Lord to use me.

"He...set my feet upon a rock, making my steps secure. He put a new song in my mouth (heart), a song of praise to our God. Many will see and fear, and put their trust in the Lord" *(Psalm 40:2b-3). (NRSV)*

It has been seventeen years now and I have been preaching and teaching God's Word in prison.

This testimony is only one of many that I can attest to of how the Lord has been using me inside these walls. Jesus began touching inmates through the Gospel and God delivered many of his people from the clutches of Satan. These treasures out of darkness are now needed in the streets, hospitals, missions and prisons.

Now that you have read Robert's testimony, let me share some of the ways that God used him while he was incarcerated in several different prisons.

Pleasant Valley Prison: Robert was in B yard from 1996-99. He served the Lord in the yard ministry there with a desire to get the gospel to as many people as possible, especially to the hard core inmates. In yard ministry he and others would hand out tracts and talk to anyone interested in the things of the Lord.

Old Folsom Prison: There from 1999-2000 where he continued to do yard ministry as he had done in Pleasant Valley.

Soledad CTF-Central: Yard ministry from 2000-2001. Here he also received his GED while enrolled in the academics class in Soledad.

Pleasant Valley: Again, yard ministry from 2001-2004.

Back to Soledad CTF – Central yard ministry from 2004-2013.

Robert writes the following: *Throughout this time of studying God's Word, praying and fellowshipping, the Lord had been using me in a mighty way in the ministry. He used me in teaching and preaching His living Word on the prison yards, in facilitating and overseeing the yard ministry, and in leading and directing yard services as a bilingual translator* and scheduling services on the yard ministry. In 2006-2009, while volunteering in the chapel library in Soledad Central, the Lord called me into a position as a deacon. I facilitated and hosted services in the chapel, praying, giving exhortations and scripture reading. At the end of the year, in 2009, I voluntarily stepped down from my position as a deacon while continuing actively serving the Lord in the yard ministry at Soledad.

Contending for the faith by practicing apologetics laid the groundwork and foundation for the Gospel that led some men to Christ as I proclaimed Jesus Christ as my Savior and Lord. Knowing why you believe and who you believe in is vital as a follower of Christ. Being confined to a small environment in the same living quarters with many different religions and sects drove me to study apologetics and to take a course from Biola University earning a Certificate of Apologetics.

I am a current participant in Criminals and Gang Members Anonymous (CGA). This is a 12-step, faith-based, self-help recovery program. Its aim is to address lifestyle addiction towards gang activity and criminal thinking. It taught me how my criminal thinking led to a criminal lifestyle that led to illegal activity. It also taught me criminal thinking and its consequences: jail, prison and a life sentence. This group has also helped me to learn that I was addicted to a certain lifestyle and criminal behavior. My alcohol and drug abuse and my self-centered actions were spinning out of control along with distorted beliefs and values. Not every criminal is a gang member but every gang member is a criminal. I have gained insight into the process of moral decision-making, behavior and action. To continue living with good, orderly direction is shown through my humble service for God. It impacted others and has impacted me and has prepared me to live an effective life as a man of God, willing to make amends to those that I have affected. First and worst are those close to me. It led me to admit there was a problem in gang affiliation. It also gave me insight respecting the sanctity of life. CGA is about undergoing a thorough transformation of character that is a journey along spiritual lines leading towards God's peace and compassion.

Change is not an overnight adventure. It is a work wrought by the Holy Spirit and through obedience. The great Apostle Paul said, "God forbid that I should boast in anything but the cross of the Lord Jesus Christ." That is all I am doing here. I am boasting about what Christ has done for me. I use my life to tell the story and to give Him glory!

Jesus loves you. Call on Him today and give Him a chance. "I will dwell in the house of the Lord forever!" Amen.

Robert Valdez in 2012, shortly before he was released from prison.

Since this was written Robert has been released from prison. California revised the "Three Strikes Law" and in the summer of 2013 Robert was released without parole. When he got out of prison his daughter was ill with cancer and on December 23 of 2013 she passed away. Robert has remained strong through this trial and is faithfully attending church and ministering the Word of God. Three of his nephews who were into drugs and gangs have come to faith in Christ since his release.

As this is written, I have just talked to Robert on the phone and he told me that he has started leading a Bible study in his apartment. Robert has been out of prison now for several years and has faithfully followed our Lord. What a great example of God's power to change a life of crime and hopelessness into a life of peace and purpose, one beneficial to one's self and to society.

As I said, for many years Robert and I corresponded while he was in prison. Every letter he sent me had written on it this verse from the Bible—the Book of Truth: **"For nothing is impossible with God"** (Luke 1:37). (NLT, KJV)

5

THE MAIN JAIL

In the late 1980's two significant things happened. First, in 1987 we lost our beloved head Chaplain, Russell Knight, to cancer. For about two years he had struggled with ill health and in September of 1987 the Lord called him to his heavenly reward. I am sure he received, "Well done, thou good and faithful servant." Upon his death, Chaplain Lile became the head chaplain at the jail and I was the assistant head chaplain.

The other significant event was the opening of our new jail in 1989. For years the jail had been struggling with the problem of over-crowding. The old jail where I started my ministry in 1976 was built to hold a maximum of 720 inmates. At the peak of our over-crowding we had up to 1400-1600 inmates. One of the tanks on the fourth floor, 4C, had 50 beds and at one time there were 126 men housed in that tank. The inmates slept on the tables, on the floor, wherever they could find a place to put their mattress.

Even with all this overcrowding there were no serious problems among the inmates. Once I heard Sheriff McKinney say to Chaplain Knight that he thought that just the presence of us chaplains on the floor had prevented inmates from rioting.

One of the ways to help with the over-crowding was to build what was called the Satellite Jail just a mile down M Street from the main jail. At the beginning, this jail housed 120 male trustees, and later the women were moved down there until the new jail was completed. On a regular basis the other chaplains and I would visit those in the Satellite Jail and we also held a weekly chapel service there.

As I said, the new jail, which was called the "Main Jail," opened in June of 1989. Now we had the Old Jail, which was renamed the "South Annex Jail," and we still had the Satellite Jail and the Branch Jail, about 20 miles west, near the town of Caruthers. The Branch Jail would be closed a few years later when our final jail was built. This jail was on the north end of the same block as the Main Jail. This jail, called the "North Annex Jail," was very similar to the Main Jail except that the housing units held 72 inmates, not 48 as in the main jail.

There was now a total of nearly 2000 inmates housed in these facilities. When the North Jail opened in the early 1990's, the Branch Jail and the Satellite Jail were closed and all of the inmates were housed in the Main Jail, the South Annex Jail and the North Annex Jail. The most inmates that we had incarcerated at one time in these jails was over 3700.

Chaplain Knight used to call jail, "The Church that God Built." Now most churches follow the command of Jesus to "go out into the highways and byways and compel them to come in," but we didn't do this. We had some very persuasive men and women in brown and blue uniforms who did this for us. And believe me, they "compelled" many to come!

We now also had a larger core of chaplains. Chaplain Lile was our Director of Chaplains. He was also the Director of Valley Missions, an organization founded by Chaplain Knight to provide funds for the chaplains' ministry. Chaplain Dixon came full-time in February of 1990 to minister to the women inmates. Chaplain Jonathan Glover came on board around this time, too, as the Main Jail was opened and we had many more inmates to whom to minister. Chaplain Ed Lee also joined our staff. Chaplain Lee was a pastor of a local church and eventually he had to resign as chaplain to devote full time to the church. Chaplain Bob LeRoy, a former correctional officer, was chaplain at the Branch Jail. When the Branch Jail closed he came in and worked in the South Annex Jail. When the North Annex Jail opened in 1994 we added Chaplain Arnie Lloyd to our staff.

Myrna – *Bible Study Coordinator*

Earlier I had mentioned that my wife, Myrna, had counseled with some of the women. About two years after I started at the jail, she would come in a couple of days a week and counsel some of the women inmates. At first, this was in what is now the South Annex Jail and later, after the Main Jail was opened, she would counsel women there.

When the Main Jail opened, our office was still in the South Annex Jail, so Myrna would walk through a long tunnel under Fresno Street and take an elevator to the sixth floor of the Main Jail.

When she first started to counsel women in the South Annex Jail, the only room available was an attorney-interview room, so she was allowed to use this room. She would have a list of women who wished to talk with her and the officers would pull them out of their tank and bring them to her.

One day Myrna counseled 22 inmates. Two of the officers went to the lieutenant and complained that she was tying up the attorney-interview room and the attorneys could not talk to their clients. The lieutenant assigned her another counseling place–a shower room! I kidded her that if one of the girls trusted Christ as Savior she could immediately baptize her!

When we got the larger staff of chaplains, we needed a secretary in the chaplains' office so Valley Missions hired Myrna as office secretary. As secretary, she not only helped the chaplains, but she was secretary for Valley Missions and coordinator for the Gospel Echoes Bible studies. She was a very busy gal. Of course, with all the office work she had to discontinue her counseling.

She worked in the chaplains' office every morning from Tuesday through Friday. She did a great job in the office until she finally retired a couple of years before my retirement.

Chaplain Flores – *Effective Ministry*

As there was a large group of inmates who were Spanish speaking, we hired a Spanish chaplain, Chaplain José Flores. He organized our Spanish volunteers and had several chapel services in Spanish. I recall that in one Spanish chapel service in our North Jail there were 140 inmates in attendance in a room designed to hold seventy-five.

Chaplain Flores became a very effective chaplain for us. He is still carrying on the Chaplains' ministry at the Fresno County Jail and the work is going well under his supervision.

One of the Spanish volunteers had an unusual story to tell. He was on vacation in Mexico and was walking down the street in this Mexican town when someone hailed him. He stopped and a man said to him, "Don't I know you?" This volunteer said, "I don't think so as I have never been here before." They continued to talk and finally the Mexican man said, "Were you ever in Fresno, California?" Our volunteer said, "Yes, I live there." "Were you ever in the Fresno County Jail?" he was asked. Our volunteer said, "Yes, l work there as a volunteer with Chaplain Flores."

"That is where I met you," the man cried, "You led me to faith in the Lord Jesus Christ while I was there!" Our volunteer continued to talk to the man and found out that he was still following Christ and that he and his family were attending a church in this town.

Chaplain Knight used to say that if God wanted someone to be saved, even in a foreign country, God would send them to the Fresno County Jail so they could get saved. Perhaps this was true, as we had an inmate from Egypt who got saved, also one from Russia and, of course, Roy from Canada and this man from Mexico.

The floors in the new jail were two stories in height, except for the first two floors, so the jail was actually ten stories tall. The first floor had the booking area and the main lobby and some other offices. On the second floor were the Captain's office, and offices for the lieutenants and all of the sergeants. This floor also had the jail infirmary and all of the medical staff and their offices. It also was where the officers' dining room was located until it was moved to the North Annex Jail.

The housing units for the healthy inmates were on floors three through six and were called "pods." Each pod held 48 inmates. There were sixteen rooms, eight on the floor and eight on the second tier. Each room held three inmates.

We chaplains and those of our volunteers who had clearance would go right into the pods with the inmates. Here we could talk to them, even sit at a table and have a Bible study with them. This was also the time when we would hand out the Gospel Echoes Bible studies and Christian literature and other books.

On the second floor of the main jail was the infirmary. Here all the ill inmates were housed, some temporarily until they recovered their health, others on a long-term basis because of their type of illness. Some of the rooms were isolation wards and if we entered these we needed to wear a protective mask as we ministered to the inmates.

Also, on the second floor of the jail was Central Control. This was a room where two officers were always on duty 24/7. From this room they could observe all that was going on within the jail and even outside. They could also remotely open the back doors of the jail. Central Control was a very busy place.

All of the pods in the main jail had one of the six pods as a lock-down pod. Inmates were all locked in their rooms and, just like I mentioned previously about our old jail, a room at a time would be let out for showers, etc. Each of these lock-down pods would also have a trustee. There was a TV in each pod and the trustee could decide which channel to watch. The rooms had three bunks and each room was usually full.

There was a lobby at the entrance of the jail off of M Street. All visitors had to come here and get a badge if they were going to enter the jail or to register if they were there to visit an inmate. There was a visiting room on each floor of the jail and those who were visiting an inmate would take an elevator to the floor they wished to visit and would step out into the visiting room. The inmate would be brought in and placed in another room and he and his visitor would converse on a telephone with a heavy glass window between them.

The first inmates who were brought into the main jail when it was completed in 1989 were the women who were transported up from the Satellite Jail. They were placed on the sixth floor. Back in the days when I first started at the jail I remember going back into the women's section in the old jail and the officers were tearing their hair out; they had 48 women in custody and didn't how they could handle so many! Now there were over 200 women inmates in custody!

The roof of the Main Jail was used as an exercise yard. Inmates from various floors and pods would be brought up on a regular schedule for playing basketball and other forms of exercise.

Around the edge of the roof were little metal rods, for what purpose I have no idea. Once an inmate smuggled a rope he had made out of sheets up to the roof and when he was able he tied the rope to one of the rods that was out of view of the officers and climbed down ten stories to attempt to escape. One of the female inmates on the sixth floor (which was really 10 stories in height) said she was looking out her window and all of a sudden there was this man looking in her window! The fellow did make it to the ground but was captured just a few blocks from the jail.

Once the new jail opened it was my responsibility to visit the inmates and organize chapel services for each floor. This kept me busy 12 to 14 hours a day. In fact, when the Main Jail opened in June of 1989, I told Myrna that I would be working 12 to 14 hours a day until at least August. I was right about the month but way off on the year as it was 1994 before I could reduce my hours to eight to ten a day.

One day a sergeant came to me and said, "Chaplain, the women in Pod A say that there is a demon in the pod." One girl would not go into her room because she thought the demon was in her room. I went to 6A and there were about five ladies there who claimed they had seen the demon. They described him as being like an opaque vapor. We sat around a table and discussed what the Bible says about demons. My special emphasis was on the fact that Jesus is stronger than demons and that demons have to obey Him. We prayed for the Lord to drive out the demon from the pod and then went to the room where the girl would not stay because of the demon. Here we had another prayer to cast out the demon from this room. As soon as I finished praying this girl went over and lay down on her bed and went to sleep! After that I heard no more of a demon being in the pod.

Was there a demon in the pod? I don't know but I do know demons are real. However, the Lord Jesus Christ has control over the demonic world and if we walk with the Lord we do not need to fear demons.

To show that when we had the Lord Jesus with us we did not need to fear demons, I used to tell the inmates the following story, which I made up: This little boy came home from school and in the course of talking to his big, 19-year old brother, he said he wasn't going to school the next day. At first he wouldn't tell his big brother why, but finally he said, "The school bully said he was going to beat me up if I came to school tomorrow." Big brother, who lifted weights and was all buffed out, said, "Don't worry, little brother, I am going to go with you to school tomorrow." Now this little guy can't wait to go to school; he hopes that bully will start something! Have Jesus with you and you don't need to be concerned about Satan. Believe me, Jesus is all "buffed out!"

The women on the sixth floor were very open to studying the Word of God. One day I went through all six pods and 20 women started the Gospel Echoes first study book, "God's Great Love." Many of them found Christ as their Savior as they studied this book. Most of these women went on to complete all four of the study booklets and earned a Bible with their name on it in gold. Many did all eight of the Gospel Echoes Studies.

Most did very well on the questions, but I remember the answer of one of the women to one of the questions. In book one, the second lesson, one of the questions was, "How many books are in the Bible?" Of course the answer is 66, but this one gal answered, "A lot!" This was technically right but not the answer in the grading manual!

Nancy – A Light in the Pod

It soon became apparent that there was just too much work in the main jail for one person. I asked one of the volunteers who was conducting a chapel for the women if she would consider helping on the sixth floor. Her name was Nancy Dixon. Nancy was a registered nurse and worked three days a week in a doctor's office. She began to come in two days a week on her days off. The women loved her, she loved the ministry and she did a great job for us. One inmate said once, "When Nancy walks into the pod, the whole pod lights up."

After several months I asked Nancy if she would consider coming as a full-time chaplain to the women. I asked her to talk to her husband, Rich, and make sure it was OK with him if she quit her job at the doctor's office and came to work at the jail. This would mean a big cut in salary for her as we had no way to pay our chaplains and we all had to raise our own support.

As I said at the time I was working 60-70 hours a week. Nancy told me later that when she asked her husband if it would be OK if she worked full-time at the jail, he said, "When he says 'full-time' does he mean 40 hours a week or the hours he works?!"

In February of 1990, she became the chaplain for the women and though it was supposed to be only 40 hours a week, Nancy loved the ministry so much that she was soon putting in many more hours. I know there were several nights when she did not leave for home until 10 or 11 PM. Nancy and I both attended the Evangelical Free Church of Fresno and the Church commissioned her as chaplain for the jail. Nancy did an outstanding job as chaplain until she left to start a recovery home for women.

One night Nancy wanted to take one of the women who had accepted Christ to the Evangel Home, a rehab home in Fresno, and asked if I would go with them to the home. It was about 11 PM, but I said, "Fine." There was just one problem, the girl's boyfriend had come to pick her up and she wanted to talk to him in the lobby before leaving for Evangel Home. This didn't sound good, but I said, "OK."

After the girl had talked to the boyfriend and he had left, we walked out the front door of the jail to go to Nancy's car which was in the jail parking lot just up the block. We had no sooner gotten out the door when who should come striding across the street but the boyfriend, and he was BIG. His arms looked the size of my thighs.

As we were talking I was afraid he would grab the girl and force her to go with him. Then I heard the voice of an angel. Actually the "angel" was Sergeant Noll. Now the sergeant was 6'4" and weighed about 250 and he even had another officer with him. Sergeant Noll said, "Any problems, Chaplain?" I said, "I don't think so, this gentleman is just leaving." I really wanted to say, "No problem now that you are here!" With that the boyfriend took off and we were free to take the girl to Evangel Home.

Now Lieutenant Martin had known we were taking this lady to Evangel Home so I surmised that he had sent the sergeant and the other officer out to make sure that all went well. The next day when I talked to Sergeant Noll he said that he and the other officer had just been making their normal rounds around the jail to see that all was well. Truly, our God's timing is perfect and His "angels" come in many guises.

Rosie – *A Bible for My Daughter*

One of the inmates who Nancy worked with was Rosie. Rosie was incarcerated in our new jail around 1990. When Rosie was a child her grandmother had taught her about God, but as an adult she had walked away from God because of all her struggles and hurts. Now she was an angry young lady, and especially angry with God, as she blamed Him for the way her life was. Because she was angry with God she wouldn't talk to Chaplain Dixon. However, her young daughter's birthday was coming and as she saw all the pretty, colored Bibles that Nancy carried in her briefcase, she wished she had one to give to her daughter for a present. To get a Bible she had to do the Bible studies and to get the Bible studies she had to talk to Nancy!

Finally, very reluctantly, she began to talk to Nancy. Then she started to do the Bible studies and she found Christ as her Savior! After her release from jail, Rosie furthered her education by getting a Bachelor of Arts degree and later a Master's degree. She also helped Nancy with chapel services in the jail and with some Prison Fellowship Seminars. When Nancy started her recovery home Rosie was one of the first board members.

Donna - *It's Never Too Late*

Following is the testimony of another of the many women who Nancy led to Christ and discipled. Donna, after her conversion, release from jail, and growth in Christ, became a staff member at NEW LIFE FOR GIRLS, a recovery program started in Fresno by another ex-inmate, Jeanne Ditto. Donna also worked as a volunteer in the jail and she wrote the following in one of our newsletters in February 1999.

First of all, I want to give all thanks, glory and honor to our Heavenly Father for having favor on my life. Born with the deadly, crippling disease of polio, I was rendered helpless from the waist down, one leg deformed and twisted.

The first twelve years of my life were spent in the hospital, having one surgery after another as doctors tried to correct and straighten my leg. I spent all the holidays in the hospital away from my family, isolated from the outside world, surrounded by other children such as myself - knowing pain and loneliness.

My family lived in Indiana and I was in the hospital in St. Louis, Missouri. My Mom was able to come see me only two times in those twelve years. I felt unloved and unwanted. There were no tutors or schooling, so I was unable to read or write very well. When I was home with my family my Mother was so afraid that I would damage my good leg that she never allowed me to do all the things my brothers and sisters did, such as riding a bike or skating.

I didn't understand as a child why I was different and crippled but the children at school made sure I never forgot it! I felt I had to prove that I could do anything that anyone else could do.

I married at age fourteen and had two children before I was eighteen. At eighteen I started experimenting with drugs and soon found myself in prison. I spent my twenty-first birthday in prison. For the next twenty-two years I was in and out of prison – spending more time in than out. I would get out for thirty days and then get sent back for another year. I did my whole parole time locked up. I refused to follow rules or regulations. No one was going to tell me what to do or where to go. If I wanted to get high I was going to do so.

My two daughters grew up pretty much as I did, alone and without the benefit of a mother. Prison was my home; I didn't care if I was locked up or not. My daughters started families of their own at an early age. I was locked up when my first grandchild was born and died.

For twenty-two years I indulged in all kinds of drugs. Prison became my home. I didn't know it then, but God had His gracious hand on me, with a plan for my life. For many years a lady named Nancy Dixon would visit with me in the jail. She would tell me about Jesus. I wanted the warm love that radiated on her face and the peace she had. The love and peace I had been searching for I found in Christ Jesus.

I now have my freedom and fulfillment in the arms of our Lord. He is replacing all the years I missed with His teaching. I can read and write. My language skills have improved. I can sit down with my grandchildren and help them with their homework and teach them the Bible. They go with me to Sunday School.

I have a clearance badge to go into Fresno County Jail and minister to the women who are in need of God's love as I was. I will spend the rest of my life teaching and showing inmates and my family the way to peace and salvation in Jesus. It is never too late to give your life to Jesus and let Him heal you and show you the way out of darkness.

I have a hunger for more of Jesus; a dream of going to Bible College. Because Jesus is walking with me I have a thirst to know and understand all His teachings. Jesus says in Matthew 11:28, **"Come to Me, all you who are weary and burdened, and I will give you rest."** (NIV)

Many more came to Christ in those years at the jail in the late 1970's and 1980's. The ministry continued to grow under the blessing of God, as we will see in Chapter Six.

Chaplain Nancy Dixon in the Fresno County Jail.

Left to right: Chaplain Davis, Mrs. Davis, Office Volunteer, Chaplain Dixon, Chaplain LeRoy, Chaplain Flores Seated: Chaplain Les Lile

Let me close this chapter with the verse Donna ended her testimony with, a verse from the Bible–the Book of Truth: **"Then Jesus said, 'Come to Me, all of you who are weary and carry heavy burdens, and I will give you rest. Take My yoke upon you. Let me teach you, because I am humble and gentle, and you will find rest for your souls. For My yoke fits perfectly, and the burden I give you is light'"** (Matthew 11:28-30). (NLT)

- 6 -

EXPANDED MINISTRY

Jesus said in the Great Commission in Matthew 28 that we were to "go and make disciples." Remember the quote from Don Hillis which I had mentioned in an earlier chapter, "Evangelism without discipleship is not evangelism." It was the conviction that we needed to do more than just get people to accept Christ that led to the development of four areas of the jail ministry.

The first area was personal Bible studies that the inmates could do on their own in their rooms. Somehow we needed to get them into God's Word on a daily basis. We found the answer in an organization in Goshen, Indiana, called GOSPEL ECHOES. It is my personal belief that this was the greatest ministry which we had at the jail. Even though I have been retired for several years now, this ministry is still going on under the leadership of Chaplain José Flores. Later I will explain more about these Bible studies.

Then we developed weekly chapel services. When I first started at the jail there were no chapel services. Several times a week Chaplain Knight would bring in volunteers who would visit the inmates in their housing units and talk to them about spiritual matters. But I felt they needed a chapel service to help them continue to grow in their Christian faith and for fellowship with other believers. We tried to get a chapel service started once, but because of classification and security reasons we were denied.

This need was met when in 1981 a group from Peoples Church in Fresno, along with Chaplain Lile, began our first chapel service. Chaplain Lile had been working as a volunteer in the jail since 1952. On Chaplain Knight's day off he would come to the jail to fill in for him. But in 1981 he retired as a chef at the Veteran's Hospital and came on full-time as a chaplain.

Every Saturday morning we held a chapel service in the briefing room on the second floor of the jail. There is not much I recall about those early chapels except that we had good attendance. I do remember that one time I was conducting a service and mentioned the "wrath of God." One of the inmates put up his hand and asked what "wrath" was. Before I could answer another inmate said, "'rath', that is something you float down the river on!"

Later we greatly expanded the chapel services. From our Christmas letter of 2008, we report that by 2008 we had over 40 chapel services each week. These were mostly done by our volunteers and we had services in both English and Spanish. At a later date one of the Catholic priests would come in and hold Mass for the Catholic inmates. One of the lieutenants told me once that at one time the chaplains' ministry had 79% of the programs being held in the jail. I was always intrigued how he came up with the figure of 79% and not 80%.

Eventually we had not only chapel services, but added what we called "Life Changing Classes." This was when we really began to make disciples out of those who had made a commitment to Christ as their Lord and Savior. These services were limited to those whom I selected and they had a Bible study format, not a worship service. At first I conducted these myself and developed the curriculum for them. Later I trained

Nancy Dixon, our chaplain for the women. As the ministry grew we trained some of our volunteers to lead these classes. Our first Life-Changing class was held in the mid 1980's and by 2008 we had 16 classes being held each week.

The final phase of our ministry growth was something which only I did and that was to conduct a true Discipleship Class. These were inmates who I selected out of the Life Changing Classes because they showed an extra degree of desire to follow and serve Christ. Bruce and David, whom we will talk about later, were in my first Discipleship Class. More will be said about this class in Chapter 7.

Though we eventually had all of the above ministries, the first was the Gospel Echoes Bible Studies. Before I explain about these studies, let me tell you how I discovered them. It was about a year or so after I started working at the jail that I first ran across the Gospel Echoes Bible Studies, and the manner in which I discovered them was rather interesting.

During my first year or so at the jail there were two Catholic chaplains who came into the jail, Father Ben and Father Gerald. I didn't know Father Ben too well, but I enjoyed talking with Father Gerald and we had a good relationship. One day, after Father Gerald had left the jail for another position, an officer came to my door with a large box of material and said, "We cleaned out Father Gerald's office and thought maybe you could use this material." Frankly, I didn't think so, but I didn't say that to the officer. I said, "OK, put it in my storage room, please, and I will look at it later."

Several days later I thought of this box of material so I brought it into my office and began to go through it. The first thing I found was material from Billy Graham, the same material that we used. "How interesting," I thought. Near the bottom of the box I found a number of Bible study booklets. I noticed they were published by the Mennonite Church and put out by a group called Gospel Echoes, not by a Catholic group as I would have surmised. As I read these studies, I thought, "Wow, these are good. I have been studying the Bible for 38 years and these help me, but they are also easy enough for a beginner to understand." Within a few days I contacted the Gospel Echoes home office in Goshen, Indiana, and ordered several copies. When they arrived I began to distribute them to the inmates and they really liked them.

There were eight booklets in the Gospel Echoes series. When one completed the first four they were given a certificate of achievement and a Bible with their name engraved on it in gold. After completing the first four there were four more studies and after finishing each of these studies they were given a certificate. Once all eight studies were completed the inmate was given a BIG certificate showing they had done all eight studies. Inmates loved to get this certificate.

Each lesson turned in had to be graded and there was a grading key furnished by Gospel Echoes. At first I graded them. One Saturday when I was grading these at the jail I looked at my watch and saw that it was ll:45 PM. This is ridiculous, I thought, I need help. I asked Helen, a lady in our church, if she would grade them. She agreed and each week I would put all the studies that had been turned in into a large packet and take them to Helen's home. She would grade them and give them back to me the next week when I brought the new lessons to be graded. If she were not home she would just leave the packet on her front porch, I would retrieve it and leave the new packet to be graded.

One week I noticed that there were a lot of studies in that packet, it really bulged. Helen was not at home so I left the packet outside her door. The next Sunday at church Helen told me that when she got the packet she dumped all the lessons out on the table and counted them and were 25! I knew then that we needed more help.

Eventually we had over twenty graders and Myrna was the coordinator. Each week she would take the lessons that had been turned in and distribute them to a grader. Most graders only wanted a few lessons as grading each lesson did take some time. You can see why Helen was a little bit taken aback when she had 25 lessons to grade! All of the graders came from churches where we could deliver the lessons each week. Many of them were from the Evangelical Free Church where my wife, Myrna, and I attended.

Myrna kept excellent records of the Bible studies. Each month she would make out a report of how many lessons had been graded and how many Bibles had been earned. Now I wish I had access to these records. There is a note from one of our newsletters which states that in February 2003, 74 inmates had earned a Bible. Glendon Bender, from Gospel Echoes, once told me that our jail used more of their Bible studies than any other jail or prison in the United States.

When we first started using the Echoes Bible studies and an inmate would finish all four books, we would notify the Echoes Bible studies home office in Goshen, Indiana. They would print the name of the inmate on the Bible and send it to us. We would then give it to the inmate.

However, we had two problems with this process. First, it took about six weeks for us to get the Bible from Goshen and many times the inmate was gone before we could get their Bible to them. At one time we had nearly 50 Bibles that we were unable to deliver. Also, the Bible which was sent was the King James Version. Now, I love the King James, was raised on it, but to give it to an inmate was like giving him the original Greek. They needed one of the modern English translations.

After a year or so I asked Glendon if we could provide the Bibles for our inmates and Gospel Echoes gave us permission. We ordered these Award Bibles from "Bibles by the Case" and there were 32 Bibles to each case. The Bibles sent by Gospel Echoes were always black, but we ordered them in many colors: white, black, maroon, blue, pink, etc. Also, we ordered them in the New International Version, which was a good modern English version, and was much easier for the inmates to understand.

Each Monday morning we would take Bibles, and a list of names to be engraved with gold lettering, to our local Christian book store. They would engrave the names on each Bible and then the Bible was taken to the appropriate inmate. They really loved to see their name in gold on that Bible. We did this for several years and then finally we had to cease putting the names on the Bible as it was just too time-consuming.

Some inmates, I know, started doing the Bible studies just because they were bored and wanted something to do. One girl wrote a poem about how she started the Bible studies just to have something to do, but about the third lesson she realized she needed a Savior and gave her life to Christ. There is power in God's Word and as these inmates would study it, many, like the girl who wrote the poem, were led to put their faith in Christ as their Lord and Savior.

The Bible–the Book of Truth–says: **"For the Word of God is full of living power. It is sharper than the sharpest knife, cutting deep into our innermost thoughts and desires. It exposes us for what we really are. Nothing in all creation can hide from Him. Everything is naked and exposed before His eyes. This is the God to whom we must explain all that we have done"** (Hebrews 4:12-13). (NLT)

DISCIPLESHIP

It was in 1989 that I started my first Discipleship Class. We met in one of the attorney-interview rooms. There were six of us and these rooms were designed for two persons so we had real close fellowship! Each week as we met we would study the Word of God, memorize scripture verses and share the struggles and victories the men were going through.

A humorous side note about the attorney-interview room is the panic button. In each room there was a button which the attorney could push in case the inmate became a threat to him. The attorney was to hit the panic button and officers would arrive promptly to his rescue. The only time it was ever used, to my knowledge, was when an inmate, not the attorney, hit it. This attorney was interviewing his client when the inmate took a swing at him. The attorney struck back and was whipping the inmate so the inmate hit the panic button!

Out of the five inmates in my first discipleship class I still remember the names of all but one. Steve was the one who I felt was the most promising. However, when he was released from jail I lost contact with him so I don't know how his walk with Christ turned out. Two others that I had good feelings about were Bruce and David. You will read about them later. Jessie was also one of the five but after he got out of jail he got into trouble again and returned to jail. Later he was sentenced to prison. I do know that two out of the five really lived for Christ, which is not a bad percentage. Bruce, whose testimony you will read later, became one of the most outstanding inmates with whom it was my privilege to work.

In the Discipleship Class we used a special Discipleship New Testament which was edited by Warren Wiersbe and designed for just such a class as this. We encouraged the men to memorize God's Word and would assign a different verse each week. The first verse they were to memorize was John 13:34-35. **Jesus said, "A new command I give you: Love one another. As I have loved you, so you must love one another. By this all men will know that you are My disciples, if you love one another."** (NIV)

David - *Could It Be Real?*

Bruce and David were housed in the same pod on the fourth floor, Pod D. David had been brought into our jail from a neighboring county and was put in 4D. David was down in the day room playing cards with other inmates when he heard someone talking about Christ. He turned around and up on the tier was Bruce telling another man in the pod about the Lord Jesus Christ. "Who's that?" he asked his fellow card player. "Aw, don't pay any attention to him. We call him the 'preacher man,' just ignore him." "You bet I will," was David's response, "I don't want any of that junk."

In a few minutes Bruce came down off the tier, introduced himself to David and invited him to a Bible study which he held in his room. "Don't hold your breath," David muttered. Twenty-three hours later David was in Bruce's room, on his knees, crying like a baby as he invited Christ into his life.

Here is David's account of his encounter with Bruce in David's own words taken from his book, *Driven by the Spirit*, and used by permission.

On one of my frequent spells in jail, I was sitting at a table playing cards when all of a sudden I heard a man shouting. It sounded like he was talking about something religious. I already had my encounter thirty years ago with a man of religion and I wanted no part of this guy.

I told the guys I was playing cards with that I was going to sock this guy up and roll him out. The guys chimed in almost all at the same time saying, "No, no, he's cool. It's just the Preacher Man." I told them mister holy-roller better not come around me or I'd knock the Preacher Man out!

What do you think happened about thirty minutes later? This jerk came up and tapped me on the shoulder. Over my shoulder I saw the hand of a black man extended towards me.

"Hi, I'm Bruce Hood. I have Bible studies every night after head count and I would like to invite you to come." He bugged me with his formality and his smiley face. I told him to get away from me. "Don't hold your breath, home boy," I said. "I won't be coming so just get away from me." Bruce merely smiled his very contagious smile and walked away.

Later that night while lying on my bunk I thought how crappy my life really was. I was beginning to think more clearly now since the drugs were beginning to leave my system. A question entered my mind. I wondered if what that Preacher Man said could be true. Many questions filled my mind that night. The next day we all got up at 4 AM, our normal time. At chow the question still bothered me. Then, there he was over at a table with four other guys. All had their heads bowed as they prayed for their food. I thought: I used to do that with my mom when I was young. Later that day I kept walking by the Preacher Man's cell and he would always be reading his black book. I started to think the guy could be for real, but he wasn't for me.

Later, after evening chow, I played cards and could hear the Preacher Man again. I acted like I was a little bothered, but I continued to play. Unlike the night before I was tuned into what he was saying. I wondered—could Jesus be real? My grandma and mom sure thought so.

The honest truth was I was sick and tired of being sick and

tired. I was disgusted with the way I had been living. I was heavy with the consequences of all I had done.

For some reason I had an overpowering desire to go to Bruce's cell. The next thing I knew I was standing in the opening of his cell. Then I heard the Preacher Man say, "What's going on?" I said, "Hey man, tell me about this Jesus you're talking about."

The Preacher Man shared a brief story from his life and then told me how he knew Jesus was real. His words penetrated my heart. I don't know how I knew but I felt he was speaking truth to me. I felt a peace in that cell while talking to the Preacher Man unlike any I had ever felt before. I fell to my knees and asked him to pray for me; I started to cry and ask for forgiveness of all my sins. The peace in my heart confirmed what I knew that in that tiny cell, Jesus had come to a broken man.

The change in me was immediate! I did not have to wait to experience God's love; I felt it right then. This spiritual touch of God left me with peace, love and joy. These were emotions I had never experienced before. I could not believe that something real actually happened to me! Most of the night I sobbed and confessed my sins. The next day the Preacher Man turned me onto some Bible studies. I stayed up twenty-four hours straight reading through parts of the Bible, filling in the Bible studies and committing certain parts of the Bible to memory.

I told our chaplain, Chaplain Glenn Davis, that I felt freer than I had ever felt in my whole life. I would not have felt any freer if I was on the outside. What God gave me those first few days was so real and complete, I knew I was going to be a different person when I walked out of jail.

After a few days I knew those other homeboys in jail would wonder if I was for real. I was going to show love to them, even though I knew there was going to be heck to pay. Sure enough, these guys started getting on me, calling me all kinds of names because I wasn't acting the same way anymore and I was carrying a Bible around. But I was committed – no more fights, no more intimidation. I stood taller. I felt like I had a new lease on life.

I had seen other peoples' "conversion" stories on television, and used to think, "You ain't nothing but a punk." I thought the God "story" was an easy way to cop out. I believed people could not handle themselves so they cried like sissies on God's shoulders! That was the way I looked at religion and God. Those perceptions had changed after my experience in the jail cell. Something had changed in me and I knew Jesus was for real.

As I began this Christian walk, the Holy Spirit revealed the truth of God's word to me. During the day I worked on Bible studies from the Gospel Echoes Association and I earned a Bible of my own.

Bruce invited me to a class offered by Chaplain Davis named the "Life Changing Class." Bruce said Chaplain Davis could really teach and make God's word understandable. He was absolutely right! What a blessing it was to be taught by such a great teacher of the Lord's word.

I faithfully attended Bible studies in jail every week. Bruce, two others and I were allowed to have a special class with Chaplain Davis each Wednesday night. The company of those men was such a comfort to me. We learned how to memorize the Bible during those sessions and this was a great time of spiritual growth.

The garbage that bound me was being washed away, slowly but surely. It was tough being a Christian at first. I had already established the reputation of being a tough guy and people knew I didn't put up with religious stuff.

When the guys got on me, it was not easy for me to take, but with Bruce's help and the other Christian brothers' help and prayers of encouragement, I was able to walk away from many potentially violent situations. After a time, I was accepted in the population as a Christian and I told many of my cellmates about God's love. I thank the Lord because without Him, I don't know if I would have made it out of jail alive.

David did make it out of jail alive. But David was a drug addict (he once told me that he felt he had used more dope than anyone he had ever met), and he and I knew that he would need help when he was released from jail. We agreed that when he was released he would go with me to the fine rehab program at the Fresno Rescue Mission.

However, there was a little problem: David had a minor charge in the neighboring county of Madera, so he was not released when his time was up, but was extradited to Madera County. Before he left Fresno Jail I did something that I did only this one time in my 34 years of ministry – I gave him my home phone number. All the other men I gave my number at the chaplains' office. But David was different and later you will see how this one act (which I am sure was directed by the Holy Spirit) saved David from going back into drugs and probably saved his life.

David and I agreed that when he got out of Madera County Jail (where he expected to be for only a few days) that he would call me and I would come and pick him up and take him to the rehab program at the Fresno Rescue Mission. A week or more went by – nothing. Then on a Sunday afternoon he called. "Chaplain Davis, can you come pick me up?" I asked where he was. He wouldn't tell me, but said he could meet me at the corner of such and such streets. I knew where that was and in fifteen minutes I was there.

There stood David with his long hair, an earring in his left ear and all his worldly possessions in a brown paper bag, but he was going to live for God! I took him to the Fresno Rescue Mission and as they say, the rest is history. David got his life on track with God and served God until his death in April of 2012.

Now, why was it so important that I gave David my <u>home</u> phone number? David later told me that when he called me he had dope in front of him and was all ready to snort some cocaine when he decided to phone me. If I had given him my office number I would not have gotten his message until Tuesday (Monday was my day off) and David would have been back into drugs and perhaps would never have become the servant of God which he became. When God tells you to do something, as He did me in giving David my home phone, DO IT! However, as I said, never again did the Lord lead me to give my home phone to an inmate.

Bruce – *I Surrender*

Bruce had been released before David was extradited to Madera County (you will read about Bruce in the next chapter), but before he left jail he and David made an agreement that someday they would return together to the jail and share their testimonies. I still remember the first time I brought the two of them into the jail for a chapel service. What a blessing to see what God had done in their lives and how they related to the inmates in the service.

As you will see in the next chapter, Bruce had a long history of drugs and crime. He was arrested, I believe, some 49 times. Once when he was speaking to the inmates in the jail he threw up his hands and said, "Men, you need to say to Jesus what we used to say to the cops, 'I surrender'."

The Bible–the Book of Truth–says: **"So now I am giving you a new commandment: Love each other. Just as I have loved you, you should love each other. Your love for one another will prove to the world that you are My disciples"** (John 13:34-35). (NLT)

- 8 -

CITIZEN OF THE YEAR

When I first met Bruce Hood, he was anything but a model citizen. Most of his childhood was spent in and out of Juvenile Hall and after he turned 18 until he was 30 years of age, he was in and out of our jail. I think he came to jail 13 times in those 12 years, maybe more. I used to kid Bruce and tell him, "Bruce, when we released you from jail we never put anyone else in your cell but just put a sign there, 'save for Bruce Hood.'" But Bruce was to become one of the greatest success stories of our jail ministry. With God nothing is impossible and <u>no one is impossible</u>.

Bruce was last arrested in 1989. Our new jail, now the Main Jail, had just opened. Bruce was on the fourth floor in Pod D. Bruce had lost everything through drugs: job, family, everything. He even sold his prized possession, a big purple motorcycle, to buy drugs. Bruce was probably the worst "crack-head" in Fresno County. When he was last arrested he was living in abandoned houses and eating out of garbage cans.

Bruce was well-known by both our sheriff deputies and the Fresno police officers. Once Sheriff Magarian asked me to come and share with all the captains in the sheriff's department about our chaplains' ministry. As I was sharing about Bruce I noticed one of the captains say something to another captain, so

I asked, "Is there something you would like to say, Captain?" He laughed and said, "I was just saying that the last time I saw Bruce Hood I was putting the handcuffs on him and putting him in the back of my patrol car."

Bruce had made a profession of faith when he was fifteen. He had been shot by a security guard at a local establishment and while he was in the hospital recovering someone led him to accept Christ. However, this made no real impact in his life and he continued on in his drug usage and life of crime.

As he grew to manhood and continued in his life of drugs, as I said, he lost everything. He was high most of the time and in order to support his drug use, he turned to criminal activity.

One time he was riding in a car with several others and he was high on drugs. When the car stopped, Bruce jumped out and was hit by another car coming from the opposite direction. Witnesses said he was thrown as high as a telephone pole. When he landed, his friends thought he was dead as they saw no signs of life in his body. They said a lady suddenly appeared and began to say some strange words over his prostrate body and they saw his chest begin to rise and fall. They knew then that he was not dead.

After his accident Bruce spent several months in the hospital. Doctors said he would never walk again, but he does walk and the only effect from this accident is a crippled right hand.

While incarcerated in 1989, Bruce finally made a full commitment to Christ as his Lord and Savior. His life was changed and he began to live for Christ in the pod. He witnessed to so many men in the pod that he was called "the preacher man."

As noted in the previous chapter, Bruce was in my first Discipleship Class and he impressed me with his sincerity and his hunger to know the Word of God. When he was to be released, I asked him to keep in touch as I really felt that he was going to do good in his Christian life. But I didn't hear from him. About ten days after his release I was talking to an inmate who had just been arrested and Bruce's name came up. I asked him if he had seen Bruce and how he was doing. He said, "Aw, he has gone back to drugs and is using again." When he said that it was just like someone drove a big butcher knife into my belly. I just couldn't believe Bruce had gone back to using.

But, as Paul Harvey used to say, "Here is the rest of the story." Bruce did use just once after his release from jail. Also, during this time a contract was put on his life by one of the local drug dealers. This, plus other circumstances, made Bruce realize that he could not make it on his own so he got into a recovery home called Second Chance. Here he got the guidance he needed to help him keep on living for Christ. Bruce became a real miracle of grace and a testimony to the power of God to change one's life.

However, I knew none of what was happening to Bruce. The chaplain for the women inmates, Nancy Dixon, had led a girl to Christ in the jail and this girl, upon release, had gotten into the women's home of Second Chance. She had been there for one year and was about to graduate and she wanted Nancy and me to attend her graduation. I still remember walking into that home and the first person I met was Bruce. I can still see the big smile on Bruce's face as I walked in and he greeted me. What a blessing to see him and to know that he was going on in his walk with Christ.

After he had completed his year at the Second Chance recovery home, had been faithful in a local church and was growing in Christ, I asked for permission to bring him into the jail as a volunteer.

One of the Lieutenants had known Bruce since Bruce was a teenager. When he heard that I wanted to bring Bruce in as a volunteer, he went to the Captain and protested. He told the Captain that he had known Bruce since he was a teenager, that

Bruce Hood was no good and never would be any good. He said, "If Chaplain Davis needs more help, let him get someone else." I believe that this Lieutenant did not know that I knew what he had told the Captain. He knows now!

But our Captain was a very wise Captain. He didn't just take this Lieutenant's word, he called me into his office and asked me about Bruce. The result was that he and Lieutenant Leonardo agreed that Bruce could come into the jail, but that I always had to accompany him. All our other volunteers who had badges to work in the jail would set the time they wanted to come in and they could come on their own without me accompanying them, but they wanted me to always be with Bruce.

The fact that I had to accompany Bruce turned out to be a blessing in disguise. As we would go into the pods half of the men in the pod would recognize Bruce as an old drug buddy. They could not believe that the man standing there in a suit and tie, carrying a Bible and talking about Jesus was the Bruce they knew. I will never forget how one man got right up into Bruce's face and said, "Hood, is that you?" He just could not believe that Bruce had changed.

Bruce had a real rapport with the inmates. He could talk to them in their own language and they would listen. Also, I think they thought that if God could change Bruce Hood there was hope for them. Our former inmates like Bruce and Rocky and others were our best workers as far as understanding and being able to communicate with the men in their situations.

One day I asked Bruce to meet me in the lobby of the Main Jail and we would go up on the floors and talk to the men. When I arrived at the appointed time—no Bruce. I waited for a while and then I asked the desk officer if there had been a young black man there waiting for me. He said, "Oh, yes, Chaplain, but the Lieutenant came in and he took him upstairs." Now this was the Lieutenant who had protested so vehemently when I wanted to bring Bruce in as a volunteer. I thought, this is interesting. When I found them the Lieutenant and Bruce were sitting in the officers' dining room having a good conversation over a cup of coffee. In the following weeks I found this Lieutenant talking with Bruce on a number of occasions.

The fact that this Lieutenant was talking so much to Bruce was odd because not only had he opposed Bruce's coming into the jail, but the first time Bruce and I met him in the jail was when we were getting on the elevator and this Lieutenant was also on the elevator. He turned a little red in the face, reached out his hand and shook Bruce's hand and that was the weakest handshake that I have ever seen in my life!

From time to time Bruce would ask me, "Chaplain Davis, when can I get my own badge so that I can come in on my own?" I would always reply, "God will provide you a badge in His own timing." Little did I know the way in which God was going to do this.

One day the Captain called me into his office and gave me a badge for Bruce and said that Bruce could now come in on his own without my having to be with him. He said that the Lieutenant had come to him and told him that Bruce was a changed man and that he deserved a badge like the rest of the chaplain's volunteers. This was the Lieutenant who had so opposed Bruce coming in! In talking with Bruce he realized that Bruce's faith in Christ was genuine and that God had changed his life. A changed life is the greatest proof of salvation.

Later, Bruce began to help me with one of my Life Changing classes. There were over twenty men in this class and Bruce was a great help to me as we sought to help them change their lives. Bruce was a living example of what God could do for them if they would only make a real commitment to the Lord Jesus Christ. When Bruce talked, they listened.

One night Bruce was late. Not knowing why he was late I went ahead and started the class. In a few minutes Bruce arrived and took a seat. However, I noticed that all through the class he didn't say a word, but just sat silent. Usually he had much to say which was very helpful, but tonight, nothing.

After class I asked him why he hadn't participated. He said, "Chaplain, when I was on the streets a contract was put on my life. One of my best friends was promised a bag of dope if he would get me to go to a certain place where some others were waiting to kill me. However, I felt something was wrong and I would not go with him. That man was in class tonight and it took the whole hour for God to get me to forgive him. But God helped me to forgive him."

Later, besides helping us at the jail, Bruce began to work at the Fresno Rescue Mission. One of his jobs with the Mission was to interview men in the jail who wanted to go to the recovery program at the Mission. If he found a man who he felt would profit from the recovery program, he would go into court on this man's sentencing day and make a plea to the judge to send the man to the Rescue Mission rather than sending him to jail or prison.

The judge that he usually appeared before was Judge Gomes, the same judge that Bruce had stood before many times himself to be sentenced. As Bruce said, "I used to stand before Judge Gomes and he would say six months or a year in jail. Now I am standing there asking him if this inmate can go into the program at the Mission."

Judge Gomes and Bruce became friends. One time Bruce was in the Judge's courtroom just to be a spectator at a trial. When Judge Gomes saw Bruce he said to all in the courtroom, "Why, there is my friend, Bruce Hood, in the audience today."

Bruce was eventually ordained as a minister of the Gospel. He started his own church where he is still the pastor. He also started his own ministry to help those on drugs, gang members, ex-inmates, etc. His ministry is called "Feed My Sheep Ministries."

"Feed My Sheep Ministries" began with a recovery home to help men get back into society as Bruce had done. It has now expanded to include training programs in graphic arts, roofing, carpet laying, auto mechanics, computer repair, graphic design, signs, banners and t-shirt making.

Bruce also has a ministry with street people and has seen many come to know Christ. Every Friday there is a food giveaway at his church. Over 250 families from the local community are served on a weekly basis. There is also a food distribution at the neighboring town of Kerman. At a special food distribution in September of 2013 over 80 thousand pounds of groceries were distributed to more than 1,500 families! God is doing all of this through a man who used to eat out of garbage cans. What a God we have!

Not only is Bruce making an impact in the community, but he has had an impact on his family. His father came to faith in Christ, as well as several brothers. Bruce had an uncle in Arizona who had been an alcoholic all his life. Bruce was asked to come to his aunt's church in Arizona and speak. His uncle came to hear him and when Bruce gave an invitation to receive Christ this uncle came forward and accepted Christ as his Savior. That has been many years ago, and to my knowledge, this uncle has never touched a drop of alcohol since and is living his life for Christ.

Read Bruce's testimony and you will see a changed life by the power and grace of our Great God.

Bruce Hood's Testimony

My name is Bruce Hood. I was born in 1958 in a little town called Caruthers. I first began to use alcohol and drugs at the age of probably about 10 years old. By the time I was fourteen years old I was already sold out to that lifestyle. I dropped out of school and just kind of lived in the streets as a street child. I was wild and rebellious. I wouldn't listen to anything good and healthy for my life; I wouldn't listen to my parents, listen to my school teachers, not even the police officers.

In fact, as I look back at my life, it resembled that man in the Bible who called himself Legion, who had the legion of devils in him. He lived in the graveyard and was daily hurting himself and that was the kind of life I lived, wild and rebellious and on drugs. I was just killing myself slowly every day, and hurting people around me, the people who loved me, like my mother and brothers and sisters, and family and good close friends.

At fifteen years old I was naturally a thief. That comes along with being a drug addict, you steal things to support your habit. There was one night I was taking a stereo out of a car. I was caught by a security guard. The security guard chased me and I ran and hid and he found me again and I jumped up and ran again. He told me to stop and I continued to run and then a gun began to fire. Well, that man shot me twice in the back with a .45 caliber pistol. I ran real hard and got away from him. This was like twelve o'clock at night and I collapsed on the back of a porch where they kept farm workers.

When I woke up it was about ten minutes 'til two and I walked a great distance to get help. There was a man coming out of a bar which was closing right at two, and he had the key and was locking the door. I walked up to him and said, "I've been shot; can you get me some help?" He called the police and they came and the ambulance came and got me to the hospital at Valley Medical Center in Fresno.

The first thing that happened as soon as I got out of intensive care was God sent Christian people by my room and they shared the plan of salvation with me. They told me that God could change my life if I would give my heart to Jesus, so I gave Him my heart. I asked Christ to come into my life right then at Valley Medical Center when I was fifteen years old.

God healed me and raised me up and brought me out of the hospital, but I started right back to the same rebellious life that I had been living. It wasn't long after that I was completely kicked out of the whole school system at Caruthers so I had to move to Fresno so I could continue some kind of schooling.

At this time I met a young lady and we ended up being married and had four children. So now I'm working and taking care of my family, but I still have a real bad drug habit. The choice of drug that I used at that time was PCP.

I became involved in illegal motorcycle racing. I had my own motorcycle and would go out and race with other men. Sometimes there would be two or three hundred of us out in the country racing, and at those races there would be any kind of drug that a person would want, any kind of sin you wanted to live in. On that Saturday I got some of that PCP drug from a gentleman. I used it and got so messed up and out of my mind that I couldn't ride my motorcycle. My brothers took my cycle and put it on the back of a truck and put me in the car with some other men to come back to Fresno. One of the men who was in the car with me told me that as I was sitting in the car he heard two voices coming out of my mouth. One of the voices wasn't me and I was saying a lot of ugly things with that voice.

On the way back we were using the same drug and these men told me this story about six months later, after I got out of the hospital. They said, "Bruce, you got so wild and so berserk we had to stop the car because you were gonna cause a major accident. When we stopped the car you jumped out and took off running like something was chasing you and you ran head on into a car." They shared that testimony with me and that there was a woman who was at the scene and two other men that I used to drink and carouse with and they shared with me too what happened.

They said when the car hit me it threw me up in the air probably about as high as a telephone pole and I came down out in the field. They said they walked over to me and my body was going in different directions and my arms and legs and there was blood coming out of my nose and mouth. About the time they got over to me they said my chest stopped moving and I quit breathing. They said right at that time there was a woman from across the street who came screaming and running and yelling and threw herself down on me and started praying and saying some strange words. They said when that happened I started breathing again and it wasn't long after that an ambulance came.

The ambulance came and got me to the hospital and the same thing happened again at the hospital.   When I got out of intensive care there were Christian people again. They came by my bed and they told me about Christ and how God loved me and wanted to change my life. Again I gave my life to Jesus and again God brought me out of the hospital. Now at this time I was in a full body cast. Both my legs and both my arms were broken.

After being discharged from the hospital and going home, as soon as I could I started that life-style again.   You can ask me why but I don't know,   that's just the type of stubbornness and rebellious lifestyle that I lived. This went on for some time. Eventually I got up and was walking again and carousing around back on drugs.

It wasn't long after that my wife left me and that was probably the thing that hurt me the most. I remember coming home, as I had been gone for about two weeks, and opening the front door and there was nothing in the house. There was not even my chair or a sheet or a bed or a spoon or a fork. That left me kind of homeless and I just kind of gave up. I didn't think there was anything to live for anymore. I really wanted to die. I wanted to commit suicide but I didn't have the strength to do it.

Again I was homeless and living on the streets. Before all this happened I had met a man named Mr. Warkentine. He used to come by our house and take me and the wife and kids to church and he would minister to us. In fact, God sent a lot of people to me, trying to get my attention before all this happened, but I didn't listen. Mr. Warkentine heard that I was homeless and out there and that the family had split up. He came and found me and kept me in a place in back of his house where he had a little shack.

Every day he would teach me the Word of God and he would work with me and take me to church. I would work around his place there but we would spend most of our time talking about the Bible. I would do good for a while and then when I would get money in my pocket I would go back out and get involved in drugs again and things like that.

Mr. Warkentine would do the same thing over and over. He would get in his car and go out in the street and he would find me and bring me back. In fact, there was one time that I was with a lot of my buddies and we were all in a place where there was nothing but drug activity going on. Mr. Warkentine walked right up in the midst of probably about fifteen to twenty people around me, all drug people. And Mr. Warkentine looked at me and said, "Bruce Hood, you belong to Jesus, get in the car."

This went on for about a year and a half, maybe two years. I continued to get involved with drugs and this and that and I was arrested for drug sales probably around the end of 1989, beginning of '90. I was sitting in Fresno County Jail and I was just so tired of the life and just thinking about everything—my family and wife and kids who meant the most to me. I was in the cell there and I was crying and trying to talk to God. I remember so many times that I went back and forth to jail and I would ask God to help me and God would help me and get me out. I was thinking about several times I went to the hospital when I was practically dead and God would always help me and bring me back to life and then I would always go and do the same thing over again.

Well, this time I was just tired and that was the time when Chaplain Glenn Davis walked by my cell and began to minister to me. It wasn't long after this that Chaplain Davis was pulling myself and some other men out of their cells and we would all go and huddle up in a little room. He would personally minister to all of us there and that's where God really began to put the devil out of business in my life.

I remember in jail I was doing Bible study through the Gospel

Echoes Team and I learned so much about the Word of God by reading the Bible and then sitting down with Chaplain Davis.

When I got released from jail I went over and started helping out at the chaplains' office. Eventually I became assistant to the chaplain there in Fresno County Jail and I was having a real good time going in and ministering to the men with another chaplain and leading men to the Lord. After some time I was able to go back into jail on my own without being supervised by another chaplain. I would go in and do the same work and it was just great being able to serve God in the same place where I used to serve the devil.

Some time went by and there was a position that came up at the Rescue Mission and I ended up becoming the senior chaplain there. So now I'm kind of working part time in the jail and then part time at the Rescue Mission, both as doing the chaplain's work. God just began to put my life together and began to use me powerfully.

One of the responsibilities I had as a chaplain at the Rescue Mission was to stand in front of the judge and ask the judge for those men who were going to the prison to come to the program. Now I am standing in front of judges who were used to sentencing me to six months here, a year there. They were really, really surprised to see me in a suit and tie and talking the way I was talking instead of seeing me sitting back there with the other prisoners wearing handcuffs and being sentenced for a crime I committed. I think that my life drew more attention to the judges, the police officers and the jailers than it did with people out in the community because they were used to seeing a wild man out of his mind, living a life away from God. Now for them to see me live for God was a whole different category, a whole different story.

For some time I continued as a chaplain at the Rescue Mission and in the jail and I would go back and forth every day reaching a lot of men for Jesus.

Some time after that I was at a pastors' prayer meeting and there was a man who sat down beside me and said, "Bruce, how are you doing?" I didn't remember him at first but he remembered me. This man was a police officer on a motorcycle and he used to chase me down on my motorcycle and give me tickets and sometimes arrest me for doing things against the law. I shared with him how God had saved me and brought me out of jail and now I was a chaplain at Fresno Rescue Mission and serving God. He shared with me that he also had given up the duty of a police officer and he's now the senior chaplain for the Fresno Police Department, saved and born again and living a radical life for Jesus.

When the meeting was over he asked me, "Bruce, how would you like to become a chaplain for the Fresno Police Department?" I looked at him and said, "I would love to but don't you remember who I am? Don't you remember all the times you arrested me?" I told him I had been arrested 49 times since I was a kid. He said, "Well, Bruce, if you want to be a Fresno Police Chaplain, I will go to bat for you." And he did. Now I'm driving a car that I used to ride in the back of, handcuffed, working with the police officers I used to run from, living a life that I didn't use to live. I'm living for God and obeying the law, whereas I used to do everything against God and everything against the law.

My life has changed and now I'm back in the community where I used to sell drugs and all these kinds of things and the people in the community were so surprised to see me. One lady made the comment, "It's a funny thing the same man who used to ride in the back of the car is now **driving** the car!" That gave me a great opportunity to preach Jesus to her and how he changed my life and how he changes everything about us, and people see that there's a great change and that there's a real God. I continued to serve God in that capacity as senior chaplain at the Rescue Mission and part-time chaplain at the jail and now the chaplain for the Fresno Police Department.

As time went by God began to call me to preach out in the community. I used to get out my old Chevy pickup, and load it up with bread and cakes and things like that at the Fresno Rescue Mission. I would go out in the community to apartments where low income people lived and give those things away.

Once I went to some apartments on Dakota, called Dakota Woods. I was giving out bread and things in the parking lot and I noticed a lot of activity going on between gangs and drug sales and all those things. After I had given out the bread and cakes I went into the office and asked the management if we could come out and do something to help and they were like, "Yes, yes, we've been waiting for someone to come."

These people gave me an empty apartment to come to and have Bible study with the adults and the children. We would give out food that we would get from the Rescue Mission every Wednesday night. Those rooms were packed every Wednesday night with people. They were not actually hungry for the food, but they were hungry for the Word of God. I was allowed to utilize the swimming pool there at the apartment complex and within a two year period I probably baptized over a hundred people in that swimming pool. We fed families, preached the gospel, and many people were saved. There are many women who came to those meetings and now are in some of the bigger churches around Fresno and serving God and working in those churches and doing a work for God.

Later we went to another apartment complex in west Fresno. We had a chapel there that we were working out of. Someone brought to my attention, "Bruce, God is building a church and we need to start looking for a church building." So we went out and started looking for a church building. We found one and this building was so bad it looked like they should have sent a missile from Iraq and put it out of its misery. It was completely rubbish on the inside and outside, condemned, had no grass, and was like a desert. The walls were all torn down on the inside, and there was no carpet, no rest rooms, I mean nothing.

But God gave me a vision for that building and I went to a

real estate man I knew who would support the ministry. He shared with me that he would get together with some of his friends and they would look at it. Well, everybody thought that I was out of my mind for wanting to take the building because it needed so much work and looked like it would never be revived. But we took the building and talked to the people who owned it and made a deal with them to restore the building and use the building for a seven year period. So we started working on the building.

There was a man and a woman who I met probably about two years prior to this at the racetrack in Bakersfield. I used to like going to the races. That was my time to get away and really enjoy some peace. I met these people who had an old custom car that they would bring to the racetrack. They would park it back in the pits and minister to the people who were racing and had cars back there, so I met them and gave them my number.

When we were building the church they called me and the man said, "Bruce, I don't know what it is but God told us to come help you with something." I told them to come on down. I was involved at that time with a lot of street outreach, car shows going on and things like that, so they came, two or three men and three women. These men were skilled at doing carpentry work, and had knowledge to build a whole house completely from the ground up. The wife of Andrew, who I met at the race track, was very instrumental in getting on the phone and calling people for donations for projects like this.

These people lived with me in my house for three months and in that time we built that church like a brand new building inside and out and the woman just stayed on the phone and talked to people about donations. She got sheet rock donated, she got carpet, windows, doors, plumbing items, tile, you name it, the whole building just came together. When we got in the middle of it there was a contractor here in Fresno who called me. He heard about it and he came by and probably rebuilt half the building himself. So the whole church came together like a miracle.

As soon as we got into the church and got started there was

a building down the street. They were building new apartments and didn't know what to do with them. He asked me what we could do with them and I told him, "I know what to do." We opened up a rehab home and that's probably been about ten years ago. Today we have two rehab homes for men and a shelter for homeless women and children, and all these people are in discipleship. They are hearing the Word every day, practicing the Word, doing Bible studies and going to church on Sundays. We are getting fruit from the vine out of these rehab homes.

It's just been one thing after the next how God has built my life. At that same church we distribute groceries to about 125 families every Friday. It's getting to be a really great thing what God is doing in the neighborhood there, reaching out to people and saving the lost. He's rehabilitating men who are on drugs and alcohol and bringing them to a life of walking with Jesus.

There are so many other things to talk about but I guess I better get ready to close it up here but I want to mention this one last thing. Out of all of the things that I've done I was able to travel some with Chuck Colson and present the Gospel and what God is doing to prisoners and how God is helping prisoners who are incarcerated. I got to travel several times in different states. (Author's note: Bruce in his humility didn't tell you that when he went out with Chuck Colson's Prison Fellowship group that he was sometimes the featured speaker).

One of the greatest events taking place since I've been saved is my family. You know, my family watched me as I was growing up in my life with Christ. It took my family probably three to four years to really believe that God had actually done something in my life and to believe that God was with me because they were used to the old Bruce Hood, the con man, lying and cheating and all these things. In fact, when I told them that Jesus had saved me the thought came to them, "What is he up to now?" My mother and my father were the two who really saw the difference in my life. My mother was one who prayed for me and when everyone else gave up on me, my mother never gave up. She always prayed and she was so grateful to Mr. Warkentine for working with me like he worked with me. She just never could stop thanking him.

So my mother and I used to meet out at her house and we would talk about God. We would open the Bible and talk about the Bible. One day I asked, "Momma, could we start having Bible Studies at your house?" She said, "Yes, you come on out and we can have Bible Study."

My father worked hard all the time. He was a junk man, and he was out in the yard and he was separating different metals and that's what he did for a living. One good thing about my mother and father, they stayed together, and they raised thirteen kids in my family. They stayed married all the way to the end and they worked hard and took care of all of us kids. So I had a great example of staying home and taking care of your family from my mother and my father. So I went out to where my father was at the bench and asked him, you know, told him, "Daddy, we're gonna start having Bible Study. Could you come, would you come to our Bible Study when we have them?" "Sure, Son," he said, "yes, you come. I'll stop doing everything I'm doing to come to the Bible Study."

Our first Bible Study we had we were in the gospel of John where Jesus told Nicodemus, "Except a man be born again he cannot see the kingdom nor enter the kingdom." My father right then gave his heart to Jesus right there at the kitchen table at my mother's house. After that we would have Bible Study and Momma said Daddy would say, "You know, Agnes, I feel so much better when Bruce comes and we read the Bible." What it was, was the word of God getting into him and bringing joy to his heart.

It was about three months later I was at church on Thursday night and my pager went off and it was 911. I called my brother and he said, "Bruce, you had better get out here. Poppa has just passed away." I rushed out to where my mother and father lived out by the Selma area. Since we had thirteen in our family and at that time Momma had 54 or 56 grandchildren, there was a big army of people out there and everybody was crying and sad.

Daddy was in his garden, plowing and getting ready to plant. Every year he planted tomatoes, cucumbers, squash and all these vegetables, and he would grow a garden. He was in his garden, plowing this row and he had a heart attack and God took him right there in his garden. My brother said when he found him that he was sitting back against the fence in the garden and he had a smile on his face from ear to ear. The first thing I thought of was he must have seen Jesus.

Momma wouldn't let the coroner or anyone take the body until I got there to have prayer. Now, at one time I was the black sheep of the family, but now I'm trusted to have prayer for things like this. So we all came into the garden, and as I was praying, reaching out and praying for Daddy, I heard a voice on the inside say, "He's in my hands!" I could hardly pray because of the excitement that was going through my bones and inside of me. I knew that God had raised me up out of those drug houses and delivered me from all this lifestyle of rebelliousness and sin. He had caused me to stand up so that my father could see what God had done in my life and could believe from seeing me and my testimony and then himself accept Jesus Christ and I felt so good even though it was such a sad time. I felt so good that I obeyed the Lord for such a time as this.

So the end of my story; it's been since the end of '89, beginning of '90 that I haven't touched alcohol. The strongest drinks I drink are coffee and Pepsi Cola, and the strongest drug I use is Bayer aspirin. I haven't taken anything from anyone else; I worked and I tried to live right the best I could. I haven't run with the crowd that breaks the law, except to preach the Gospel to them. God delivered me completely from those lifestyles and set me free and called me to stand on my feet and represent Jesus in this same community where I used to represent the devil.

Lastly, I want to say the first time that I was arrested I was probably about 13 years old. My first arrest was for stealing the judge's bike in Riverdale, a little town near Caruthers, and my last arrest was for assaulting a police officer. It wasn't

really assault; I was just kind of resisting arrest and it turned into kind of an assault. I want to say again I've been arrested 49 times, and you know for sure that God would choose the foolish things of the world and use those people to confound the wise. God bless you and this is my testimony and thank you.
Pastor Bruce Hood, Feed My Sheep Ministries

Did you notice the title of this chapter? "Citizen of the Year." Each year United Way and another organization in Fresno give an award to the person in Fresno who has given the most back to the community. Many are nominated for this award and several years ago Bruce won this award. Truly our God is the God of the impossible.

Bruce also was recently given an award by the U-Turn Program. In their magazine they said this in their write-up of Bruce:

Bruce works with Prison Fellowship, giving his testimony and being a spokesperson for Fresno Innercity Outreach, Inc. He has also been involved with Fresno County jail inmates by making countless court appearances as an advocate for inmate release and inmate transition to recovery programs.

Pastor Hood is well-known throughout Central California for his tireless work in bringing the Word of God, helping the hungry, providing housing, rehabilitation, in custody services and job network services to those individuals on parole and probation. He has received many awards and recognition for his service to the communities of Central California.

Thank you, Bruce, for being a shining light for those in the darkness.

This award from U-Turn was presented to Bruce by the Sheriff of Fresno County, Sheriff Margaret Mims. Sheriff Mims was raised in the same town as Bruce, Caruthers, California. She went to school with Bruce's older sisters and she knew what a wild person Bruce had been. I am sure she also knew that Bruce had spent 13 years going in and out of her jail! How fitting it was that she presented this award to Bruce.

Chaplain Davis (center) with Bruce Hood (right) and David (left).

Did you notice that I said that when Bruce was last arrested he was living in abandoned houses and eating out of garbage cans? September of 2013 Bruce's Feed My Sheep Ministries distributed 80,000 pounds of food at Kerman, a town near Fresno. Only our God can take a man who was eating out of garbage cans and use him to feed hundreds of people.

Even though I am no longer in Fresno, Bruce and I are still in contact and he is still being greatly used of God. Several times I have said that if Bruce were the only one that we reached through the jail ministry that it all would have been worth it. Of course, there were many more and you will be reading the testimonies of Rocky, Greg, and others. Our God is a God who changes lives.

For over 25 years Bruce has been a faithful servant for the Lord Jesus. Jesus, in one of his parables, told about a faithful servant. The Bible–the Book of Truth–says: **"The master was full of praise, 'Well done, my good and faithful servant. You have been faithful in handling this small amount, so now I will give you many more responsibilities. Let's celebrate together'"** (Matthew 25:21). (NLT)

- 9 -

SAVED, BUT
BACK IN JAIL

As you read in the previous chapter, some of those who were saved in our jail we brought back later as volunteers. We had many volunteers (as I recall at one time we had 78 volunteers conducting the various services), but some of our best were the ex-inmates. These men and women had been there, done that and were able to relate to those still incarcerated.

These volunteers had to be trained in how to conduct services in the jail and in jail security. Some time in the 1990's we joined with Prison Fellowship and used their training courses to train our volunteers. The Area Director for Prison Fellowship was Rev. Austin Morgan. Austin was a good friend of mine and one of the finest men I have ever known and with whom I've had the privilege of working. Sadly for us, Austin went home to be with the Lord in 1999.

After Austin's death he was replaced as Area Director by a man who was saved in our jail. Joe had done some time in prison and after his release he became Austin's assistant. He is still serving as Area Director for Prison Fellowship.

Not only did we have volunteers who were able to get badges to come in and conduct services, but the jail allowed me to bring in guest speakers. These were sometimes pastors, but more often we would bring in former inmates. We found that the former inmates had a greater impact on the men and women than did even the pastors. I would go to Lieutenant Leonardo and give him the information on who I would like to bring in and he would approve or disapprove. In those days an ex-inmate could come in if he had been "clean" for one year and off of probation and parole.

Raphael – *Send Me Back to Prison*

One of the inmates that I brought in was Raphael. Raphael had an interesting story. He had accepted Christ as his Savior while he was in prison, and for two months before he was discharged he immersed himself in the Bible. He thought he was so strong as a Christian that he would never go back into drugs.

When he left prison and got on the bus to return to Fresno, he said that there were only six other people on the bus and they were all addicts! All they talked about was dope and living the life of an addict. Raphael said that when he got to Fresno his nose was running from all the talk about drugs. Twenty minutes after he got off the bus, he was over in the old Lazy 8 Motel shooting drugs.

After three days he was miserable at the failure he had been as a Christian so he turned himself into his parole agent. He hadn't reported yet as he was supposed to do, so he was in violation of parole. He told his agent, "Send me back to prison. I can live for Christ in prison but I can't live for Him on the streets." However, he had a wise parole agent. Instead of sending Raphael back to prison he sent him to a rehabilitation home run by a former drug addict. Here he got his life straightened out and was able to live for the Lord.

Barry – *A Long Rap Sheet*

Another ex-inmate who I brought in to speak in a chapel service was Barry. We had a very interesting night that night, but before I tell you about that let me tell you about Barry before he became a Christian.

Barry was raised in a Christian home but he got in with the wrong companions and into drugs and crime. He was one of the first men who I met when I started working at the jail. He would talk to me and he had personal sessions with Chaplain Lile also, but there was no real change in his life.

Barry was a big fellow, about 6'3" and weighed about 250 pounds. One day he had an altercation with one of the officers and from that time on he was "high power." This meant that he was dressed in a yellow sweat shirt (the other inmates wore red), and whenever he had to go to court or a visit, he was escorted by two officers and shackled hand and foot.

After he was released from prison for the last time Barry found Christ as his Savior. Barry started attending a good church in Fresno and after he had been out for over a year and was off parole I asked Lieutenant Leonardo if I could bring Barry in and have him share his testimony in a chapel service. Permission was granted.

Very clearly do I recall the night I brought Barry in to speak in the chapel service. When I brought a guest in with me, we would go to the officer in the main lobby and I would tell them that Lieutenant Leonardo had granted permission for the guest to come in. The officer would check his list and there would be the OK from Lieutenant Leonardo. The guest would then leave his driver's license as identification and was given a visitors' badge to wear. We would then take the elevator to the floor where the chapel service was being held.

The night I brought Barry in Lieutenant Martin was in the lobby. This was the only time I ever saw him in the lobby when I was bringing in guests, but God had a purpose in it. I still remember the lieutenant staring at Barry and I knew he was trying to remember where he had seen him. Of course it was in jail!

Barry went with me upstairs and we had a great service. He really was able to relate to the men. After the service, as I was taking Barry back downstairs, an announcement came over the PA system, "Chaplain Davis, call such and such a number." I knew this was the lieutenant's number and I knew what he wanted! After I had taken Barry back to the lobby and he had left the jail, I didn't call the lieutenant's number but went to his office.

Though this incident happened many years ago it is as clear in my mind as if it were yesterday. The lieutenant had Barry's "rap" sheet (his list of crimes) spread out on his desk, in fact, it covered the top of the desk and went partway down one side. As I sat down he leaned across the desk and said, in a rather stern voice, "Do you know who you brought into the jail tonight?" I didn't tell him that Lieutenant Leonardo had approved Barry coming in, though he should have known that. Instead I said, "Yes, but let me tell you about Barry."

So I told the lieutenant how Barry had gotten out of prison and that he had gone back to using dope. He had been out only a few weeks when some drug dealers came to him and wanted him to be their "enforcer" (I told you Barry was a big man). He was to deal with anyone who crossed the dealers in any way. The dealers told Barry he would have to get off the dope if he was to work for them. To me this has always been a little ironic, if you want to work for a dope dealer, you can't use dope.

Barry decided to go up in the mountains and kick his habit. As they walked out of the door he told his wife, "Grab that Bible." His wife told me later that what he said really shocked her. "If he had said, 'Grab that dope,' 'grab that piece (gun),' that would have been normal, but 'grab that Bible?'"

That night up in the mountains, after the children had gone to sleep, Barry and his wife sat around the campfire and Barry began to read the Bible. As he read he began to cry and he was crying so profusely he couldn't read so he told his wife to keep on reading. As she read, the Holy Spirit worked in Barry's life and he gave his life to Christ – he was born again!

After they got back home and the dealers came to him, Barry didn't tell them he had become a Christian but gave some other reason for not working with them. He still wasn't a strong Christian. However, I recall Barry telling me that when his old friends came by and used foul language that it really bothered him and he had to tell one of them to leave because he couldn't stand the language he was using. Eventually they quit coming to his house.

Barry got into a good Bible-preaching church in Fresno and began to grow in the Lord. He got a good job which was a miracle for someone with as many felonies as he had. On your job application you have to check if you have ever been convicted of a felony and Barry checked the box. During the interview one of the interviewers asked him to tell them about the felony. Barry thought he would just tell them about some minor felony (he had a lot to choose from!), but God said, "Tell them about the last one." The "last one" was attempted murder. Barry told them about this and he said that up to this time all five of the interviewers had seemed to be very attentive, but now it seemed like they were not listening. Barry got the job and in six months was promoted to foreman.

As I shared this about Barry, Lieutenant Martin reached over, picked up the rap sheet, tore it in half and threw it in the waste basket. He said, "If you are satisfied, I am satisfied."

Barry served with us for a number of years and then moved to Arizona. He came back one time as a volunteer with the Bill Glass Weekend of Champions and that was the last time I saw him. Recently I talked with Barry on the phone, and he said he was ministering in the local jail where he was living.

Rosemary - *I Can Walk Straight*

Another of our ex-inmates who became one of our volunteers was Rosemary, who was led to Christ through the ministry of Nancy Dixon. Before coming to jail and finding Christ as her Savior, Rosemary ran a gay bar in Fresno. She always carried a .38 caliber pistol with her. It was like an American Express card, "She never left home without it." But then, if you are carrying a .38, who needs an American Express card!

Rosemary was faithful in her ministry at the jail. She said to me one time, "Now when I go to jail I can walk straight up." Finally, her health began to fail, but she would still come to visit us in the chaplains' office until the Lord called her home to her heavenly reward.

Ron - *Put Your Faith in Me*

Strictly speaking, Ron was not one of our volunteers. When I first met Ron he was Chaplain of Juvenile Hall in Fresno, but he also came into the jail to minister to various inmates.

Ron was an ex-drug addict and was saved when he was loaded on drugs. Ron said he came home one night, loaded as usual. Ron had said that he could kill anyone as long as he had a good enough reason and God would justify it. When he came home that night he had made a list of the people he was going to kill.

That night when he came home, though he didn't know it, his wife had made up her mind that when Ron went to sleep she was going to take their young daughter and son and leave Ron. However, she went to sleep before Ron did.

Ron said he couldn't sleep so he got in his car and drove out into the country. There, parked under a tree and loaded on drugs, he heard a voice say, "Put your faith in me and not in the needle and I will do it for you." He said that he chose to believe that it was God speaking to him and he gave his life to Christ. His commitment was real and after some time he became chaplain at Juvenile Hall in Fresno. Periodically, as I said, he would come and visit inmates in the jail.

Before coming to Christ Ron loved two things: he loved his drugs and he loved to fight. He was always getting into altercations in the bars or wherever he was. But let him tell you in his own words what God did in his life.

Ron's Testimony – *I Forgive You*

"I forgive you," the little girl told me. "You are not the same man who shot my daddy. Jesus has made you different."

The night that I asked Jesus to come into my heart, I knew that I was sorry for the things that I had done, but I had no idea how sorry I was until eight months later at the end of Junior Church when I had to tell that little girl that I was the man who shot her daddy in the face during a bar fight on Christmas Eve. I was shaking and crying and praying under my breath, "Lord, please just take me now. Don't make me have to be in front of this little girl anymore."

A horrible wave of guilt and shame swamped me while that little girl was hugging me. I remembered God's Word in Isaiah where it said that Jesus bore the shame and guilt of the sins of mankind. I realized that day what it cost for God to save us. When Jesus went to the cross it cost Him infinitely more than anything else He could have done. It wasn't just the physical pain of the cross that He endured, but it was the suffering of bearing our guilt and the shame of our sin that cost Him so much. I had done many wrong things, but it felt as if just that one sin of shooting that little girl's daddy was going to kill me and Jesus had borne the guilt and the shame of all of my sins. Oh, wow!

That was the first day that little girl had attended our church and that was the day she accepted Jesus as her Savior.

God changed me when I was an undesirable sociopath into a man who loves Jesus whole-heartedly.

I was not raised in a Christian home. The extent of my religious education was that God was a "pretend guy" who kept you in line whenever your folks weren't around.

Carol, my wife of 49 years, married me when we were 17 and 18 years old respectively. By the time I was 24 we had a son and a daughter. I also had a police record and a $100 a day heroin habit.

In December of 1974, in a local parking lot, I heard a former crime partner tell his friend, Larry, that God loved him just the way he was. He said that if you opened your heart to Him, God would change your life. I watched Leroy as he talked to Larry. I thought that this guy looks like he believes what he is saying. When he talked, he spoke with authority – like he really believed it. If there was a God and He could love Larry and Leroy, then maybe He could love me, too.

It was sometime after this encounter that I gave my life to Christ, parked under that tree, as Chaplain Davis has said.

The road to recovery was physically and emotionally painful. After three years I surrendered to God's call to ministry. With only a high school diploma from Clovis Adult Night School the prospect of further education was discouraging. However, after taking 12 units my first semester in college to see if success was possible, God enabled me to finish nine years of college work in six years. I obtained my Master's Degree in 1982 from California State University, Fresno, and I obtained my license as a clinical psychotherapist from the California Board of Behavioral Sciences, also in 1982.

Now I am the director and chief clinician for the Counseling Resource Center (CRC) in Clovis, California. I also hold licenses and certificates in several specialty fields, including critical incident response, stress management, grief therapy, marriage enrichment, anger management, communications, drug and alcohol addiction and time management.

Also, I am the head chaplain for the Fresno County Probation Department Juvenile Division. Here I supervise 17 *chaplains and over 300 volunteers. Our work with juvenile offenders through a military-style boot camp, annual three and four-day camps and an extensive mentoring program has resulted in a recidivism rate as low as .08 percent.*

RON'S MESSAGE TO ALL IS THIS:

There are people who live all around us and they are dying and going to a Christless grave unless we tell them about Jesus. We not only have the responsibility, but we have the privilege, of being able to do that.

People become more willing to talk and to be in a relationship when they know you want to hear about them. Find something that you like to do and use it to share Christ with the people who like to do the same things. Find something in common with somebody and you will find opportunities to share Christ through that commonality.

Our sharing Jesus has been God's only plan from the very beginning. He does not have a Plan B and He uses the most unlikely, the most undesirable folks, to carry out His plan. I count it a privilege to share Christ and I just wish that everybody else would see it that way.

Fred – *God's Ways Are Not Our Ways*

Fred, another of our volunteers, was not saved in our jail, but he came through our jail. He was an inmate in Fresno County Jail in the early 1970's, which was before I started working there. Following his trial Fred was given a prison sentence, and he left to serve his prison time.

In prison he joined the Aryan Brotherhood (AB), a notorious prison gang. One day Fred's cell was left unlocked as a black inmate was being put in the cell next to him. Fred grabbed his "shank" and ran over and stabbed the man several times. Why? As Fred told me he didn't even know the man; the man had done nothing to Fred. He stabbed him simply because he was black.

Six months later, Fred was subpoenaed to Los Angeles County by a friend of his who had disposed of the weapon he used in the previous incident by bending and wrapping it in toilet paper, and flushing it down the toilet. While at the L. A. County Jail, Fred was allowed to go to the law library where inmates worked on their legal documents. He went for the sole purpose of using one of the phones that was in the room.

Each time he used the phone, there was a leader of a black gang that the AB was warring against using a phone at the same time. That individual always had his crime partner with him, sitting on a trash can about five feet behind him. Fred said, "Wow, I have access to the leader! If I kill him, I will have made my name! I would be respected and can live out my time in prison, resting on the laurels of that victory!"

The third time Fred went to use the phone he took a knife that he made by sharpening a piece of metal on the concrete floor. He attacked the leader, stabbing him once. He then turned and stabbed the crime partner once and then returned to stabbing the leader three more times. Today, Fred praises God for the leader's crime partner hitting him in the head with a typewriter. That stunned Fred to where he dropped the knife. The leader picked up the weapon and stabbed Fred 10 times. The last two times, he stabbed him in each eye while Fred was lying on his back. All three went to the hospital with Fred staying for a month and a half.

While at the L. A. County Hospital the room that Fred was in faced west. One day Fred shared this, *"I was looking out the window and to my amazement there wasn't any smog over the city and no fog over the ocean. I saw clear blue water and even saw Catalina Island. Wow, this is what I am missing! I said out loud, 'Had I died in this fight the fellas at San Quentin and Folsom would have talked well about me for a few days and then would have forgotten about me.' I said, 'You watch, Fred, when you return to San Quentin you will receive a hero's welcome.' Sure enough! When I got back to San Quentin and was walking down the tier to my cell I heard, 'Right on, Fred, you were awesome! You did great!'—etc., etc.! So, God was working on me at that early stage."* That is what Fred shares regarding his last incident that nearly ended his life…but for the Grace of God!

Fred continued to associate with the Aryan Brotherhood until one day, as he told me, he was sitting on his bunk and realized that life as he was living it was meaningless. He was sick and tired of the way he was living. As he thought about his life, he became depressed because he saw no future. But sitting on that bunk that day, Fred gave his life to Jesus Christ as his Lord and Savior. He said a peace came over him such as he had never known before.

This conversion and regeneration of his dead spirit came at the same institution where Fred had killed his victim. So, he killed a man at CIM, Chino, California, and then six years later officials sent him back to the same prison (and to the same building) to receive his spiritual life. Fred acknowledges that "God's ways are not our ways."

His commitment was real and eventually even the prison guards saw the change and moved him into another part of the prison, away from the Aryan Brotherhood. Eventually he was paroled. He became a volunteer with us and worked with us for a number of years at the jail. He is now working with Prison Fellowship in Fresno and still works as a volunteer at the jail.

Several of these ex-inmates who became volunteers in the jail are still continuing to minister in the jail. Some have been doing it for years.

Rocky - *Broken Habit*

One of the most outstanding of our ex-inmate volunteers was Rocky. The following was in our newsletter the summer of 2006: "Two new classes have been started recently. Rocky, a former inmate now working as an associate chaplain, has started a Recovery Class in the North Jail for those wanting to overcome their drug addiction. The class uses a special 'recovery' Bible which utilizes the Christian 12 Steps and is an excellent resource for those wanting to overcome addictions of any kind. The class also uses study material prepared by Prison Fellowship especially for this class. Rocky, once an addict himself, is now helping others break the habit."

Once Rocky was speaking to a group of inmates and he told them his name was in the Bible. In Matthew 13, Jesus said some of the seed fell on "rocky" soil. You will read his testimony in the next chapter.

The Bible–the Book of Truth–says: **"What this means is that those who become Christians become new persons. They are not the same anymore, for the old life is gone. A new life has begun"** (II Corinthians 5:17). (NLT)

- 10 -

GANGS TO GOD

"What's Rocky Martinez doing inside the jail?" This came from our new Captain at the jail. This was his response when he saw one of our volunteers, Rocky Martinez, walking down the hall, getting in the elevator and going up to one of the floors. If he had seen Rocky locked up in the jail he would not have been surprised, but Rocky walking around free inside the jail?! He couldn't believe it.

Let me tell you a little bit about Rocky (you can read his own testimony later) and then we will come back to this incident with the Captain.

Rocky was a Bulldog, a notorious gang in Fresno, actually named after the Fresno State sport team, the "Bulldogs." Rocky's street name was "Vicious" and he lived up to his name. One time I asked Rocky, "How many fights have you been in, Rocky?" He replied, "Probably 200." "How many did you lose?" I asked and his reply was, "Maybe 20." You didn't mess with Rocky.

One time Rocky and his girlfriend got into an argument and she locked him out of the apartment. He went out to his truck, got a crowbar and smashed down the door! That was Rocky, violent (I think he used the word "crazy" one time to describe himself), in and out of prison, given over to drugs and the gang life-style. By the way, I used to tell this story but I had it a little wrong. I said that Rocky used his chainsaw to cut down the door, but it was just a crowbar. You have to admit, the chainsaw story is a little more dramatic!

One time Rocky was locked up in our old jail (now the South Jail) and he was TV monitor. That means that no one changed channels without Rocky's permission. But one fellow did. Rocky became enraged, grabbed a sheet and wrapped it around the man's throat and if the other inmates had not intervened he would have strangled the man. He would have killed a man just because he changed a TV channel. That was Rocky's mentality before he met Christ, but God saved him and he became one of our best volunteers, a <u>changed life</u> by the power of God.

The Captain did not know of Rocky's conversion, so when he saw him inside the jail, he got one of the sergeants and said, "What is Martinez doing inside the jail? The last time I saw Martinez I was waiting outside his house on a stakeout to arrest him when he came home." The sergeant said, "I don't know, Captain, all I know is that Chaplain Davis got permission for him to come into the jail and minister to the inmates." The Captain said, "Before Martinez leaves you bring him to my office, I want to know what changed his life." Incidentally, this shows how well known Rocky was to the police. This incident had happened several years before, but our Captain still recognized Rocky.

The Sergeant brought Rocky into the Captain's office and Rocky was able to tell him that it was the Lord Jesus Christ who had changed his life. He told him that he was no longer a Bulldog and getting into trouble with the law, but he was now a law-abiding citizen, living for the Lord. As he left, the Captain said, "If you ever have any problem with any of the jail staff, just tell them to come see me!"

The power of a changed life is the greatest testimony to the power of the Gospel.

Rocky not only helped us in the jail and was very active in his church, but he started a recovery home for addicts and was very successful in helping many ex-inmates get back into living successfully in the community. He also taught classes inside the jail, including a recovery class. He is still teaching this class and ministering in the jail.

One incident that Rocky told me about shows how God changed him from "Vicious" to "Victor." Sometime after his conversion and after he had dropped out of the Bulldog gang, he was picking up his son from school when he spotted a car parked across the street. He recognized those inside the car and knew they were gang members coming to confront him, and perhaps beat him up, for dropping out of the gang. Now Rocky had done this very thing to others when he was a Bulldog, but he never did it in front of the victim's family and here were these men confronting him in the presence of his little son. This angered him and the very fact that they were there to confront him angered him more.

His first thought was, "I will get to my car and get a tire iron and defend myself." I guarantee you that there would have been blood on the street and it wouldn't have been just Rocky's. But God spoke to Rocky, "Do this my way." So Rocky got into his car with his son, the men approached the car, and following God's leading, Rocky began to share his testimony and how God was changing his life. After a few minutes the gang members looked at each other and without laying a hand on Rocky went back to their car and left. After this Rocky had no more trouble with the Bulldogs. When we do things God's way He will work on our behalf.

Rocky's Testimony
Vicious to Victorious

I came from a family of 15 (11 brothers and 4 sisters) where drugs, alcohol and gang involvement were the norm. I was born in 1959 to migrant workers who were hard workers and loving in their own way. By the time I had come into this world, though, my parents had already become immune to the madness. My early years of childhood were not very pleasant.

I was befriended by an elderly neighbor who brought me gifts and clothes only to take advantage of my youth. He molested me one year over and over until my older brother found out. After that all hell broke out at home. I remember crying and being so scared as my older brother and his friends were terrorizing his family with acts of violence. I hid in my mom's closet shaking like a leaf while hearing my brother's voice saying aloud, "Where is he?" When he found me there in that closet clinging to the top cupboard I remember the beating I took. I was only six years old and from then on my life changed completely.

I was weak so my brothers had to toughen me up like them. They taught me how to fight, steal and other things in the school of hard knocks. I was arrested at nine years old for being in a stolen 1964 Chevy with some older guys from the neighborhood where I was raised. Then came drugs, alcohol and joining my street gang. There I learned more about crime and violence until I was arrested and sent to the California Youth Authority. By then, at 16 years old, I had already done heroin and cocaine on a regular basis and experimented with every other drug known to the addict.

I cursed God daily for the way I turned out, blaming Him for the madness and chaos of my life. Jail and prison followed for the next 17 years. During those years I remember how angry I was and how much I hated this world in which we live. Being prejudiced, racist, perverted, violent and lost, there I was looking through the eyes of a madman. Looking back now, no wonder I couldn't find anyone to fill the void that I felt in my heart.

Relationship after relationship always ended in disaster. I had two sons in these relationships, Rocky and Sonny. Rocky went home to be with the Lord in 1997 after a long illness with heart problems, and Sonny, well, he just learned to despise me because of my life-style and not ever being there for him.

I remember in 1983 sitting in the county jail of Fresno awaiting trial on two "assault with a deadly weapon" charges over a drug deal gone wrong. I was facing multiple years in prison again. I remember this guy from Victory Outreach coming to the jail and talking about Jesus. Brother Roy Deleon would come weekly to our unit and preach about Jesus Christ. At first I just sat around looking at some of the guys who would go to the bars to listen. I always thought that people who walked around with Bibles were weak and no good. One week, though, I remember one of the guys coming up to me and saying Brother Roy wanted to talk to me. He talked to me about knowing my older brothers, Big Joe and Jerry (Cobra). He told me that I reminded him of them and he could see me in prison the rest of my life if I didn't change.

I went back to my cell that night and then beat up a guy in our unit the following morning for calling me weak. No one said I was weak after that! When Brother Deleon came again he led me to Christ. I didn't feel any different, though, but the seed was planted.

I started doing the jail Bible studies and talking to the chaplains, Rev. Lile and Chaplain Davis, whenever I could. They were always there for me although I didn't see it at the time. I was released shortly afterward because no one showed up in court. I do remember, though, sitting in that holding cell next to the courtroom and praying for this God, whom I had never seen, to help me. Anyway, I went to church but soon fell away and then I remember the pain all over again.

My first marriage crumbled. My father passed away. I got back into drugs and committing crimes again to support the madness of addiction. It was during this time that I first started thinking about ending my life. I guess jail would have to save my life again because I sure couldn't.

In 1986, I got out of jail again and went to stay with

my younger sister, Mollie. She introduced me to a friend of hers who would later become my wife and support me in tough times. Sylvia is still my wife today and she showed me love and helped me to fill that void I felt in my heart. Even though I would go to prison in 1988 for drug sales she stayed by my side. We had a son together whom we named Samuel.

My Mother, who would pass on to be with the Lord while I was in prison, had told me at a visit that she did not think she would make it this time around. I remember looking at her from the other side of the glass and seeing that she was looking much older. Through sober eyes a tear began to roll down my face. I remember telling her not to say that, but looking down at her sweet and beautiful face with the long gray hair I realized some truth to her statement. It would be the last time I would see my Mom and the feeling I get every time I remember that day always brings the tears. My Mom was very special to me because she was the one woman who never gave up on me or stopped loving me even in my addictions and madness.

When I was released from prison in late 1990 I remember my wife Sylvia coming to pick me up at Corcoran State Prison. I had made many promises to her while in prison like most of us prisoners do - changing my lifestyle, getting a job and working to better our relationship as a family, etc., etc. I must have written a couple hundred letters from prison with these promises. After a short time out of prison I remember her one day bringing a shoe box to me filled with these letters and telling me to take back all of my lies because that's all they were. I began being abusive to her, living my lies all over again.

I was in and out of jail and prison for violations again and in June of 1992 I was arrested for my fourth DUI. While in jail for this charge God began dealing with me like never before. Sylvia asked for a divorce and told me that she didn't want the kids (she had two children, Melissa and Danita, when I met her) seeing me behind bars anymore. She was pregnant, too, at the time, but didn't tell me about it because of all the hurt I *had caused her and the kids. I would not see or hear from her again until my sentencing date in October of 1992.*

Imagine the surprise I got when she did come to visit me so I could see Samuel before I went to prison again. There she was with child and a big manila folder with the divorce papers. She would not speak to me either. I told her that I loved her and her reply was, "Just leave me alone then."

Through this time in jail God had begun tearing down some walls around my heart. After eight years of running from God's calling in my life I began to realize that God's love had never failed me through it all. Remember, I said earlier that being locked up always seemed to save me. Well, I know now that God used the system to save me from my madness. There in the county jail I repented of my sins and asked God to come back into my life.

When I went to my sentencing date in October 1992, I had written a letter to the judge and asked him to consider me for a program to help me with my drug and alcohol problem. The DA's office and the probation department were totally against it, but God had other ideas. He touched that judge's heart that day and I know that today without a shadow of doubt. I was sentenced to a Christian rehabilitation home in Madera, California, for one year.

I remember thinking about this place in Madera where God was allowing me to go while I was awaiting my release from jail. I thought it was going to be a cakewalk with all the Christians giving in to my needs. Boy, was I in for a big surprise! Upon my arrival I immediately learned the word "NO" for just about any request and also to pray about it. The men there were cut out of the same cloth I was, lost and confused and bound by sin. It was tough, and a lot of times I felt like God had set me up for failure. With so many feelings of anger and resentment I began to rebel against God and the leadership in the Home. I was constantly in trouble and was given extra work assignments and scriptures in the Bible to write over and over.

During this time God had began working on my marriage to Sylvia. She was very supportive of me in spite of the hurt I had caused her and the children. On January 19, 1993, we had our second son, Gabriel. I was able to be with her at the hospital for the delivery. It was the first time in my life that I had been free to see the birth of one of my sons without being incarcerated. That really meant a lot to me at the time because, looking back now, it helped me to realize that I needed to grow up and start being a real father and husband. God's grace would have to be with me here in this matter because I never knew how to do either.

While in the home one day, after having another bad day and allowing Satan to deceive me again, I decided to leave and just go back to prison. I left one Sunday morning shortly thereafter. I got a call from the pastor who was in charge of the Home. He listened to all of my complaints and then said to me, "Rocky, the real problem here is YOU!" He told me how much God really loved me and that I had to stop listening to that voice that was always speaking bad things into my life. The devil, that's him, is always taking what he can from God's people. He prayed for me and then told me that I needed to turn myself in to parole as soon as possible. The next day I called Pastor George and asked him if he would drive me to the parole office.

As soon as I got there I was placed in handcuffs and told to sit down and was asked why I left the Home. I replied, "I just don't know how to deal with life and changes." After speaking to the pastor, my parole officer told me that he would be willing to send me back to the Home if I wanted, but that I could not do this again.

I went back to the Home and was told that I would have to start all over again and that I was being placed on discipline for my actions. I was given a hula hoe and told that I would have to clean up the weeds on the canal bank for the next 30 days and stay away from all the other brothers in the Home. I *was left out in the sun daily to complete the task alone.*

One day, though, I'll never forget, that was the day God used those weeds on the canal bank to set me free. Some of those weeds were like small trees with deep roots. As I was hitting, kicking and trying hard to pull one out, I heard a voice calling me by name. At first I thought it was one of the brothers playing games with me. I went out looking down the grape vineyard rows for this person but found no one. So I went back to work and no sooner had I started on those weeds when I heard my name again. Hitting, kicking and trying hard to pull out that big weed with roots I heard that voice again, saying, "That's how hard it is to pull the anger and the madness out of your life, Rocky."

You see, there was always this voice telling me to do all these bad things because of my sinful nature and surroundings. But there on that canal bank God's voice became so real to me and changed my life completely. He restored my marriage to my lovely wife and friend, Sylvia. He gave me a chance to be a real father to Samuel and Gabriel and my two step-daughters, Danita and Melissa. But, most importantly, He showed His love and mercy for me, a sinner.

Today I am living a life that is so much better and worth living. God saved me and set me free from all the madness and chaos simply by me asking Him to come back into my life. Thank God for second chances.

If you don't have a personal relationship with the Father in Heaven right now, I encourage you to just say these few words to Him: "Father, please forgive me of my sins and help me to know you in a personal way. I love you, I need You and I want You to guide my life forever. Amen."

Note: Rocky's wife, Sylvia, went home to be with the Lord on November 3, 2017, after suffering with cancer for more than a year. Rocky was her faithful caregiver during her illness. Today Rocky is serving as a missionary in Uganda.

After Rocky had finished his term at the rehab home he returned to Fresno to his wife and family. He got a job as a gardener and after a short time had his own business. Once when I was on vacation I had him come out and do my yard work in the mobile home park in which we lived.

Now it so happened that a retired lieutenant from the jail also lived in the park. While Rocky was pruning the bushes in my yard this retired lieutenant happened to walk by. He stopped to talk to Rocky and he said to Rocky, "You look familiar, have we met before?" Rocky told him that they had met in the jail but now he was living for the Lord. This was a testimony to that retired lieutenant that God can and does change lives.

Remember that verse that Robert would always put on his envelope, Luke 1:37: **"For nothing is impossible with God."** (NLT) You may feel that there is no hope for you, but just as God changed Robert, Bruce, Rocky and many others, God can change you.

The Bible—God's Word of Truth—says: **"But God's truth stands firm like a foundation stone with this inscription: 'The Lord knows those who are His,' and 'Those who claim they belong to the Lord must turn away from all wickedness'"** (II Timothy 2:19). (NLT)

Again, the Bible—the Book of Truth—says: **"...those who become Christians become new persons. They are not the same anymore, for the old life is gone. A new life has begun"** (Second Corinthians 5:17)! (NLT)

Rocky Martinez in 2011

- 11 -

PARTNERS IN MINISTRY

In chapter two, I mentioned my close friend and co-worker, Austin Morgan. When Prison Fellowship (PF) decided to have an Area Director based in Fresno several men, including myself, were chosen as a committee to work with the supervisor of all Prison Fellowship Area Directors for California to choose a man to be Director for the Fresno area.

There were several applicants for the job and we were told that each would give his qualifications and background. The leader of our group would then question each and based on their answers we were to give them a grade from 1-5.

Austin was my good friend and I knew that I was biased towards him so when he would answer a question I would give him a lower grade than I might have given to someone else. When all the points were tallied Austin had the most votes of any of the candidates, however, I had given him less points than any of the other men on the interviewing committee!

Prison Fellowship had a good training program for volunteers and we began to work with them in the training of our jail volunteers. We would schedule these sessions several times a year. At first Austin and I did the training and then one of our ex-inmates began to help Austin. After the Lord called Austin home to glory, Monte, another of our volunteers, took over the training sessions and he did an excellent job.

But we had other ties to Prison Fellowship. Three of the inmates who were saved in our jail became associated with PF. Two of them became Area Directors for PF; another worked for a number of years with "Network for Life," the follow-up ministry of Prison Fellowship.

Another prison ministry that we worked with was the Bill Glass Prison Ministry. Bill Glass was a former National Football League player and is in the Football Hall of Fame. After he retired from football he began to do city-wide evangelistic campaigns at the urging of Billy Graham. Then he developed a prison ministry where he would bring well-known Christian athletes into the prisons for a weekend crusade. These athletes would share their testimonies and many prisoners were won to Christ through these services.

For many years we would host a "Weekend of Champions" on an annual basis. We saw many come to Christ and many of our own volunteers were involved in the weekend ministry. There were several of the "champions" who came to our jail that I particularly remember.

Paul Wren was a weightlifter and at one time held the title for lifting the most pounds in three weightlifting categories— the squat, bench press and dead lift, a total of 2342 pounds. This record stood until 2004.

Paul could tear a telephone book in half starting on the back side of the book. Also, he would pick out the heaviest officer and let him jump off a chair onto his stomach. Paul said one time a man jumped off the chair and missed his stomach and cracked some of his ribs. So he told the officer, "If you miss my stomach I get to jump on your stomach!" The officer never missed!

Jack Murphy, "Murf the Surf," came in every year with the Bill Glass Team. In his early years Jack ran with quite a few Hollywood celebrities, including the Gabor sisters. He is best known for stealing the Star of India sapphire out of the American Museum of Natural History. At the time this was known as the "Jewel Heist of the Century." He was successful in getting away with the sapphire but was captured two days later and the gem recovered.

Jack later turned to other crimes and ended up in prison in Florida. He recalls the time when he was an inmate and Bill Glass came into the prison. One of the speakers was Roger Staubach, quarterback for the Dallas Cowboys. He said that Roger took off his Super Bowl ring and tossed it out in the crowd for the men to see. When Jack got a hold of it he said his heart started pumping very fast. Here he was a notorious jewel thief with this big diamond ring in his hand! Roger did get it back!

While in prison, through the ministry of Chaplain Max Jones and the Bill Glass Crusade, Jack became a Christian and upon his release from prison he joined the Bill Glass Team and became one of their staff.

Perhaps the "champion" whom I related to the most was Ernie Shavers. You sports fans will remember that Ernie was a heavyweight boxer and fought Mohammad Ali for the heavyweight championship. Ernie was known as the hardest hitter in boxing. Ali said that when Shavers hit him that he shook up all his kin folk in Africa!

But the reason that I remember Ernie Shavers was not just that I recalled his exploits as a boxer, but he was a distant relative of Joe Louis. When I was a boy Joe Louis was my hero so it was special to me to meet someone related to him.

By the way, I heard the fight that Joe Louis had with Max Schmeling the second time when he knocked Schmeling out in the first round. We didn't have a radio at the time so we went to our neighbor Obie's house to listen to the fight. I was only seven years old, but I remember as Obie was inviting us in he said that we were too late and the fight was over. My heart sank, but of course he was just kidding and we did get to hear the fight, all two minutes and four seconds of it.

Monty Christensen was another ex-inmate who now has his own prison ministry, and he, too, came to our jail to hold services. The first time that I met Monty was when we went to a Network for Life conference sponsored by Prison Fellowship. Monty was the featured speaker. However, the first night he did not speak, but they gave each of us a copy of his autobiography, "70 x 7 and Beyond."

After the service, when we had gone to our room, I began to read his book. It was so interesting I couldn't put it down. Finally, I had to go to bed with the book half finished.

In his book he began by telling about his conversion to Christ. He had just gotten out of prison and he had gone to visit his 77-year-old uncle with the purpose of robbing him. He found such love and acceptance from his aunt and uncle that when his uncle told him about how Christ loved him and died for him, he trusted Christ as his Savior and he didn't rob his uncle!

Monty's life didn't immediately straighten out. He tried to live for the Lord but soon drifted back into the old ways and was back in prison. This happened to him several times. He would go to prison, get back in fellowship with the Lord and vow to live for Christ, only to get released and go back to the old life style and back to prison.

As I was reading this book l remember thinking, "I don't want this book in my jail. I don't want the men I lead to Christ to think that they can keep on falling back into the old way of life." Then I suddenly realized something, this was exactly like some of the men that I was dealing with and they needed to know that even if they fell numerous times that God would forgive them and they could become victorious in their Christian walk just as Monty eventually did.

On the back cover of the book was a picture of Monty, a nice looking, clean shaven man. At the service the next morning, I was sitting next to this stranger with a big, full beard. The speaker finished several minutes early and he told us to turn to the person next to us and introduce ourselves and spend time praying together. Imagine my surprise when this bearded fellow beside me introduced himself as Monty Christensen!

When Monty spoke at the jail he told us how he was arrested one time in his home state of Montana. He said the cops were waiting at his home to arrest him when he returned home, but he spotted them and took off at full speed in his car. The officers gave chase and shot his tires out and he careened into a mobile home park. He said that what saved him from getting caught was that a man in the mobile home park ran out to see what was going on and he had a rifle! When the police saw the rifle they turned their attention to him and Monty got away.

A group of hippies were having a party in a park up the road and he joined the party. When the party broke up he asked a girl if she could give him a lift out of town. She said, "Yes," he got into her pickup with her and another girl, and they started down the highway.

All of a sudden cops were everywhere. As Monty said, "There were police from all over the place, even the local dog-catcher was there." The police called over a loud speaker for the girl to stop and she began to cry, "What is wrong? I wasn't even speeding." Monty said, "I think it is me they are after."

Another person I remember quite well and who had a tremendous message for the inmates was Sandi Fatow. She has been billed as one of the most exciting speakers at the Bill Glass "Weekend of Champions." I have been in services with Sandi when she was speaking to our women inmates and there was not a dry eye in the group. Sandi wrote a book entitled, "Smokin' and Jokin.'" She said when she started into drugs all she wanted to do was, "smoke a little, joke a little, and have some fun." She never dreamed she would end up in prison, but this is Satan's way; he entices you to have a "little fun" and then he ruins your life. Jesus said, **"The thief's purpose is to steal,**

to kill and to destroy. <u>My purpose is to give life in all its fullness</u>" (John 10:10, underline is mine). (NLT)

For a time Sandi lived in the fast lane, partying with others in the drug scene. Through her drug usage she ended up in crime. Finally arrested, she spent much time in prison. The last time she was released from prison she was sent to a Christian half-way house, much against her will. There she found Christ as her Lord and Savior and her life was changed forever by the power of God. Sandi and her husband are still traveling across America sharing the good news that Jesus saves and changes lives.

A group from GOSPEL ECHOES, the same organization from which we got our Bible studies, also came and ministered in the jail. This group, led by Rev. Glendon Bender and his wife, Lorna, presented a gospel music package which the inmates greatly enjoyed. Many men and women found Christ and a new way of life through their ministry. The inmates looked forward to the services by these outside groups and individuals.

In Christian service it takes teamwork, everyone working for the same goal. The Bible–the Book of Truth–says: **"The ones who do the planting or watering aren't important, but God is important because He is the one who makes the seed grow. The one who plants and the one who waters work as a team with the same purpose. Yet they will be rewarded individually, according to their own hard work. We work together as partners who belong to God. You are God's field, God's building - not ours"** (First Corinthians 3:7-9). (NLT)

The Harvest Team from Gospel Echoes Team in 2015
Left to right: Glendon, Lorna, Kristi, Jordan, and Sawyer Bender,
Titus Bowman, and Delbert Yoder

- 12 -

LITTLE THINGS

Someone wrote: "Shamgar had an ox goad, David had a sling. Dorcas had a needle, Rahab had some string. Samson had a jawbone, Aaron had a rod. All of these were little things, but all were used by God."

Two "little things" that I found effective in the jail were humor and bookmarks. The practice of telling jokes came about very naturally, I like to tell jokes! But I found that humor had a place in my jail ministry. Jail can be a very depressing place for those incarcerated, and a little humor could go a long way to lessen the stress. Some men came to listen to me as I talked in the pods in order to hear a joke, but they ended up listening to God's Word.

Andy was an example of this. One day as I was sharing with a group of men in one of the housing units in our North Jail several were asking questions and we had a good discussion on various Bible subjects. As the group dispersed I noticed Andy standing off to one side and I said to him, "Do you have a question, Andy, or is there something that I can help you with?" He said, "No, I was waiting to see if you were going to tell a joke!"

Sometimes we take ourselves too seriously. Now we need to be serious about serious things, but we need to also lighten up at times.

Humor was also a way that I could relate to the officers.

One of the officers and one sergeant in particular used to share jokes with me.

Once as I was eating lunch in the officers' dining room this sergeant stopped at my table. He said, "Glenn, did you hear about the old mountain boy who came down out of the mountains to celebrate his 40th birthday? Well, he got to celebrating a little too much and an Arkansas State Trooper pulled him over for speeding. The officer walked up to the car and said, 'Do you have any ID?' The old mountain boy looked at him for a moment and then said, "bout what?'" The sergeant was halfway out of the room before I got it!

A similar story that I used to tell was about the policeman who, late one afternoon, stopped this young guy for speeding. The officer walked up to the car and said, "I've been waiting for you all afternoon." The guy replied, "I got here as fast as I could." They said when the officer stopped laughing he told the young fellow, "Get out of here, but slow down." Supposedly this was a true story.

Jokes about people standing at the gate of heaven to see if they were permitted to enter I did not use because no one gets to heaven by their works. However, there were two such jokes that I did use.

One was this fellow was standing at the gate of heaven and St. Peter said to him, "Why should I let you into heaven?" The guy said, "Because I am a good man and have done many good works." So Peter said, "OK, tell me about your good works, but let me warn you that in order to get into heaven by your good works, you will need to score 1000 points." This fellow said, "No problem," and he began to tell Peter all the good things he had done. He was a good husband, a good father, a good church member, gave lots of money to the church, and on and on he went. Finally he said to St. Peter, "How many points do I have?" St. Peter said, "Five." The guy exclaimed, "Only five and I need 1000! Why, if that is the case no one will ever get into heaven but by the grace of God." St. Peter said, "Bingo."

So before I would tell this joke about someone standing at the gate of heaven I would always explain that we could not work our way to heaven but we could only get there by the grace of God. I'd tell them that He sent Christ to die for our sins and that we needed to accept Christ as our Savior in order to enter into heaven.

It seems this man was standing at the gate of heaven and St. Peter said to him, "Man, we don't know whether to let you in or send you away. It is touch and go, can't you tell me something that would tip the scales in your favor?" So the guy told St. Peter the following:

"You see, I was driving down the highway and I saw these four bikers harassing this poor women. I stopped my car, went to the trunk and took out my tire iron. I walked over to the leader of the group, a big brute, bulging muscles, tattoos all over him, and a big ring in his nose. I pulled that ring out of his nose and raised my tire iron and said, "You leave that woman alone or you will have to answer to me."

St. Peter said, "Wow! That's impressive. When did this happen?" The guy said, "About two minutes ago!"

One of our lieutenants was a no-nonsense, retired Navy man but even he had a sense of humor. One day I needed to ask him a question, so I went down to his office. His door was open and he was sitting there behind his desk. I stepped inside and said to him, "Are you free?" and he replied, "No, but I'm reasonable!"

Even some of the civilians who worked at the jail had a sense of humor. One of the officers once asked one of these civilians, "How long have you worked here?" The man replied, "Ever since they threatened to fire me."

The other "little thing" that I found to be effective was bookmarks. Now these were nothing but bookmarks on copy paper which I made myself. It started when I made up bookmarks to help the men after they left the jail. There were a number of churches in Fresno that had recovery programs for addicts and I made up bookmarks with their addresses and phone numbers. These I would give to men before they were released so they could call the church and attend the classes.

One bookmark in particular that I remember was one I made up to connect men with Bruce Hood's church and recovery homes. Bruce called his ministry, "Feed My Sheep Ministries," so I had a picture of Jesus, the Good Shepherd, holding a little lamb and then the information to get to Bruce's church and the phone number to his recovery home.

The men liked the bookmarks so much that they wanted one even if they weren't being released! So I began to make up bookmarks with Scripture on them. Each bookmark would have a special, selected Scripture. As I prayed and meditated on the jail ministry, God would put certain Scriptures on my mind and I would make a bookmark with this scripture on it. One scripture that I used a lot was Isaiah 8:11-13: **"The LORD has said to me in the strongest terms: Do not think like everyone else does. Do not be afraid that some plan conceived behind closed doors will be the end of you. Do not fear anything except the LORD Almighty. He alone is the Holy One. If you fear Him, you need fear nothing else."** (NLT)

Another bookmark had a picture of Jesus and then the Bible passage, John 14:1-6. We would talk about how Jesus talked about heaven, how he promised to return, and that He was the only way to heaven. In John 14:6, Jesus says, **"I am the Way, the Truth and the Life. No one can come to the Father except through Me."** (NLT) As one commentator has said about this verse, "Jesus was either a lunatic, a liar or Lord; He leaves us no other choice." Believe me, Jesus is Lord.

Another bookmark that I handed out a lot was what I call the Romans Road of Redemption. These verses showed the steps to becoming a child of God (see Appendix A, pg. 165). There were six verses in the book of Romans that I used to explain the way of salvation. I would encourage the inmates to believe these verses, meditate on them, memorize them and share them with others.

To show that when Christ really comes into our lives God no longer wants us to sin but to live for Him, I made a bookmark with II Timothy 2:19 on it. **"But God's truth stands firm like a foundation stone with this inscription: 'The Lord knows those who are His,' and 'Those who claim they belong to the Lord must turn away from all wickedness.'"** (NLT) God loves us and wants what is best for us so that is why He wants us to turn from the old ways and to live His way. His way is best.

There were many other bookmarks that I used. One had a picture of Jesus and the scripture from Ephesians 1:9-10: **"God's secret plan has now been revealed to us; it is a plan centered on Christ, designed long ago according to His good pleasure. And this is His plan: At the right time He will bring everything together under the authority of Christ – everything in heaven and on earth."** (NLT)

The Bible says that God had this plan in mind before He created the world and it says that Jesus will return someday and God's plan will be fulfilled. You are in God's plan. He wants you in His family and to reign with Christ forever. You can become part of God's plan by making Christ your Lord and Savior (see Appendix A, pg. (165).

When I would enter a pod, men would come up to me and want a bookmark. Before they were given a bookmark I would share the meaning of the verse written on it. Little did I realize when I began to hand out paper bookmarks that it would be one of the best means to spread the Word of God in the pods. I found out that inmates would take anything that was free, even if they didn't need it!

Before I left the jail ministry, I had over forty different bookmarks which had been distributed by the dozens to the inmates. God has said that His Word will not return void. I believe many lives were touched by these bookmarks.

Humor is wonderful, but eternity is no laughing matter. Jesus said in Matthew 25:46 that some **"will go away into eternal punishment, but the righteous will go into eternal life."** (NLT) The Bible says that we can only become righteous in God's sight by believing in Christ as our Lord and Savior, **"All who believe in Him are made right with God"** (Romans 10:4b). (NLT) To believe in Christ doesn't mean to just believe facts about Jesus, but to make a commitment to Him as your Lord and Savior, and decide to live for Him the rest of your life. Read Appendix A (pg. 165) and make sure you are truly saved and are a child of God.

The Bible—the Book of Truth—says that we must make a choice: **"But if you are unwilling to serve the LORD, then <u>choose today whom you will serve</u>. Would you prefer the gods your ancestors served beyond the Euphrates? Or will it be the gods of the Amorites in whose land you now live? But as for me and my family, we will serve the LORD"** (Joshua 24:15, Underline is mine). (NLT)

PRISON TO PULPIT

"Your son is dead." Those were the chilling words that the parents of Greg heard over the phone one night. The police had arrested Greg and thought he had died. He was taken to the hospital and there he was revived. Or was he really dead and God brought him back to life? Who knows? Just remember the Bible says in Luke 1:37 that NOTHING is impossible with God.

Because of his crime Greg was brought to our jail. I visited Greg and shared the scriptures with him and he received Christ as his Savior. He began to read and study the Bible and grow in the Lord.

Greg received a prison sentence of several years and when he went away to prison I lost track of him.

Several years later Tony, one of our volunteers, asked me if I knew a Greg Runyon and I said that I did. He said that when Greg got out of prison he began to attend their church. Greg had gone to Bible school and this coming Friday night he was being ordained into the Gospel Ministry. Did I want to come? You bet I did! I went to the service.

Greg didn't know that I was coming to his ordination service. As I was sitting in the audience and he was up on the platform, he suddenly saw me. He came down off the platform and gave me a big bear hug! When it came time for the laying on of hands to ordain Greg, I was invited to participate. What a thrill and what a testimony to the power of our Great God to change lives.

Greg's Testimony

Early Life

I was brought up in a home where we went to church on Wednesday night and both Sunday morning and Sunday night. My parents tried to raise their children with Godly values and a faith in Jesus Christ.

My upbringing was a very typical one in many ways, with a father who worked hard and a mother who also worked hard raising their three children. We lived a very good life which I would describe as upper middle class bordering on wealthy. I was the oldest and had a sister named Kym, who is five years younger than me, and another sister, Cyndi, who is almost ten years younger than me. Dad was a very successful Real Estate broker and also was involved in politics in the city of San Jose, while my mother gave up her teaching career to raise us children after Kym was born in 1968; Cyndi came along in 1973.

We were an all-American family to those who saw us from afar, but inside the house there were problems. Dad had issues with drinking and they took a toll on me, but he loved me and tried his best to be a good father and I do not blame any of my behaviors on him. He has made significant changes in his life, too. Mom was believed to be a godly woman by almost everyone who knows her. She is a strong woman who was faithful and true in times of great trial and never gave up on me.

In fact, one time when I was a teenager and Dad was out of town, I was out partying and came home to hear her praying for me. I went upstairs and demanded that she stop being so loud and that she quit praying for me. Her response is a classic one. She said I could ask her to pray softer but that she would never stop praying for me until I stopped doing what I was doing and gave my heart to Jesus. She never quit praying for me and I know that her prayers were answered on May 19, 2001, in the jail at Fresno County.

I do not wish to glamorize any of my sinful actions nor do I wish for anyone to think that my desire is to dwell on anything other than the powerful Grace and Redemption of my Savior Jesus Christ. I do want to give a small background into my actions prior to accepting Jesus, so what follows is a very brief overview of what led me to meet the man who was always there to tell me that Jesus was loving me and wanted to see me succeed outside jail – Chaplain Glenn Davis.

I began to drink in 1978, which is right around the time my father, after having been elected to the City Council in San Jose, California in 1976, was forced to resign after his drinking had caused two very public and embarrassing incidents with the police. I was in eighth grade and I used to steal booze from my parents' liquor cabinet and take it to school in containers that I hid in my locker. Between classes I would take a couple of swigs to get me into the mood to deal with some of the issues my father's resignation caused. When he stepped down, many of my teachers said words to me that should never have been said. I was 13 and people called my dad names to my face that I know would not have been said to his face. Anyway, I started to drink because I thought that it would help me deal with the pain my father's drinking caused. Crazy how we see people fail in areas and then believe that we are more powerful than those who have fallen. Sin is like this: it fools us into thinking that the failure of others to control it is because they are weak and that we can control it. Sin MAKES US WEAK and the only way to control sin is to be in the Arms of Christ and remember that when I AM WEAK, HE IS STRONG.

By the time I entered High School I was in trouble, and within two years and two different schools, I dropped out of school taking the Proficiency Test which is similar to a diploma. I drank too much, cut school, gave up on Athletics (I played all three sports – Football, Basketball and Baseball), and began to use and deal in cocaine by the time I was 17. I thought that I was such a big-time player and for about a year I was, but my family caught me one day with drugs and things went downhill fast after that. I was clean for about six months but then I began to use drugs in a very destructive way.

Rather than pay for the cocaine with money I earned I began to steal from my father. I stole a great deal of money from my family over the next five years, probably close to fifty thousand dollars, if not more. When I first took money from them, they did not prosecute me, but after two or three years of my promising to stop, going to rehab at Teen Challenge and then falling back into my addiction, they called the authorities on me. So in 1987, after I committed more crimes against my family, I was sent to County Jail for six months. I then was given an opportunity to serve my sentence at Work Furlough, but I walked away from there, stole a car and was sent to State Prison in 1989.

Prison

From 1989-1995 I was in and out of prison three times, once on a parole violation for drunk driving and twice for selling drugs (Methamphetamine). I was very hardheaded and thought that sin was fun. I also was not the smartest criminal. In fact, after I was saved, a police officer I went to church with stated that smart criminals are tough to catch, that is why they caught me so often!!!

In 1993 I was released from Susanville State Prison to Fresno, where my parents had just moved. I also received a large settlement from a personal injury lawsuit of about $60,000 when I came home. It took me four months to party my way through that money and by the time Easter arrived I was broke and unable to pay rent for my apartment, so I decided to sell methamphetamine to make ends meet. This was a horrible decision and within six months, I was back in jail and found myself in real trouble.

However, God was working in my life. A man would come to the jail and every time he came into my housing area the Love of God shown through him and I could not help but be drawn to his side. Chaplain Davis shared with me that my incarceration did not have to define me. God had a bigger plan for me and Chaplain began to share with me the truth of being forgiven through Jesus Christ. During this time my interest in being a Godly man was intrigued because when I was a young man, I had felt a call from the Lord, but I had run from His calling and frankly was still running when I met Chaplain Davis.

When I first met Chaplain Davis it was in 1994. I was in jail, having been arrested for selling methamphetamine and for violating my parole. This was a very tough time for me because I also had squandered $60,000 in less than six months. The money was from a settlement stemming from an auto accident that I was injured in. I had partied and wasted that money and now I was sitting in a jail with nothing to show from all the "fun" I had, but a certain prison sentence and a ton of shame over my behavior. I knew that this time my sentence would be for a significant amount of time. After all, I had been released on Parole in November of '93 and here it was a year later and I am back in jail with new charges involving the sale of drugs.

I was anticipating doing at least three years and thought I might have to do up to six years, so my mental state was not positive and, frankly, my thoughts were very dark and included the thought of ending my life. Actually, a few days after being arrested I was placed on suicide watch after I told a deputy that I felt like I did not want to live anymore. It was a week or so following my time being observed in suicide watch that Chaplain Davis entered my life.

Chaplain Davis entered my housing unit with a smile and a message that life was not about being locked up, it was about being free, free not only physically, but more importantly, being free spiritually. He shared with me that my book was not yet written because the Lord had a plan for me. His love and enthusiasm for Jesus were so clear and powerful that I began to believe that God could and would forgive me. He was so warm and genuine that I knew I wanted the relationship with God which he demonstrated, a relationship built on real truth rather than feelings or words. Chaplain Davis visited with me at least once a week and soon I found myself studying the Bible and I began to see changes in my life. In fact, big changes were right around the corner.

My case did not resolve itself for almost a year and a half. During that time something tragic, miraculous and amazing took place. I was moved to a cell and my cellmate was someone who I knew from the streets and had, in fact, sold drugs to. Frank was looking at a long sentence for two bank robberies he perpetrated. The sentence was for 16 years and he was struggling with the fact that his grandfather was dying. Frank knew he would not be able to see, touch or hug his grandfather whom he loved and who loved him deeply. Frank was hurting far more than I knew.

One morning I heard a faint, "Help me, Greg," and when I looked down, Frank, my "cellie," was lying in a pool of blood. He slit his wrists and sliced his veins in the crook of his right arm. He had lost so much blood that he had thrown up and he was turning gray. Normally when an inmate attempted to contact an officer to come to their cell it would take about five minutes. This is due to the fact that it involved an intercom and once that was answered an officer had to descend from the control tower to open the outer door and then the cell door. On this day someone answered within 10 seconds and once they heard my pleas for help, an officer arrived within a minute and medical help arrived within three minutes! I tied off Frank's wounds and stayed in his blood while the medical workers took precious time to put on gloves so that they would not be contaminated by his blood. I, however, did not care about that, I was trying to save a life. At one point I slipped in his blood and ended up damaging my knee substantially, so much so that for the remainder of my time in County Jail I was housed in the infirmary. Thankfully, Frank pulled through and I was told later that he made it with only 2-3 minutes to spare. He lost over four pints of blood and just barely survived. It was a miracle that things worked out the way they did, and I was later given a reduction in my sentence due to the "heroic" nature of my actions that morning. The reason I share this story is that because of this event I met my wife, Catherine, who was the neighbor of Frank's girlfriend. More about that later…

Turning Point

Chaplain Davis would visit me in the infirmary after I saved Frank's life and he was so kind, warm and loving when we spoke that I knew God wanted me to return to Him. I reached out to God while in jail, but looking back it is clear to me that I never truly gave my life to Him until that day in May of 2001. While I went through this time of going in and out of jail, Chaplain Davis always showed me the love and devotion I needed. He shared with me that God's plan for me was far greater than being an inmate in the prison system. How right he was…

My wife, Catherine, came into my life soon after the incident with Frank. She lived next to Frank's girlfriend and one day, as fate would have it (we know it was the Lord), Catherine happened to answer the phone. Hearing her voice gave me a jolt and soon after speaking with her for the first time I began to frequently call her and we developed a friendship over the phone for 5-6 months before we ever laid eyes on each other. On the day we first saw each other we both knew how special our relationship would be.

Without going into every detail, we were married on January 20, 1996, and on January 22nd I was arrested and sent back to prison because of my using drugs and violating the terms of my parole. Over the next five years I went back to jail four times and Catherine suffered each time. There were many awful experiences and I promised to change countless times, only to fall back into the habit of drugs. I also was physically threatening to her and on more than one occasion I slapped, pushed, or hit her.

Catherine lost most of her vision in 2001 due to an infection in her eyes, and I chose to continue doing/selling drugs rather than provide her the care she deserved, and I sank deeper into my addiction. Finally, she had enough in 2001 and she said that if I did not shape up and get clean and sober, she would not be with me. In fact, her exact words were, "I love you enough to die for you, but I do not love you enough to go to hell with you." It was a moment that changed my life, because the events that followed were difficult and produced challenges for us both. However, the plan the Lord had was about to come into play...

In May of 2001, after being arrested at gunpoint by my parole officer and three police officers, I was told that Catherine was blind and that I was believed to have physically been responsible. Hearing that someone felt I was capable of hitting Catherine and beating her to the point of her losing her sight angered me and I began to yell at the parole officer.

It was at this moment the Lord God intervened and the truth of my condition hit me. Not only was my wife in bad shape physically, I was in a spiritual spiral leading me far away from God and the truth of his Son. God's power and Spirit hit me and I literally began to sob over Catherine's suffering and the truth of my behaviors.

Seeing my sincere remorse, my agent had compassion and wrote a report that allowed me to be released in only 80 days rather than getting a new criminal charge. On the way to the jail, the transporting officer, having heard my conversation with Agent Gipson, shared with me that the thing I needed to do was give my life to Jesus Christ. This officer told me that he had lost his wife because of his gambling addiction and that through Jesus they had reconciled. He told me that my wife would likely come back to me if my life showed the imprint of God's Spirit. In other words, he shared that there is nothing impossible for God, and that God would give me the desire of my heart if I truly would delight in Him according to Psalms 37:4. He prayed with me and dropped me off at the jail...

So, the following night I cried out to the Lord in my cell asking Jesus to not only forgive me, but to take my life so that I could live the life He wanted me to live. I prayed for almost 30 minutes and when I was done there was a freedom and peace that can only come through the power and presence of God.

I thank God for those two men, and I was blessed to have had a relationship with my Parole Agent upon my release that would best be described as a friendship. In fact, one day he came by my school so that I could pray with him. When I discharged my parole, he came and gave both Catherine and me a big hug and told us he knew the Lord was in our life because of how dramatically we had changed.

Pastor

After being saved in 2001 we joined Harmony Free Will Baptist in Fresno where the entire church treated Catherine and me with warmth and kindness. In fact, one of the men who opened his heart to me was Fresno Police Chief Jerry Dyer. He became one of my friends and also, more than a friend, he is my brother. I still call or text him a few times a year to keep in each other's life. He has been a great friend and mentor to me. We have wonderful memories of the church there and the time we spent there.

Since 2001 I have earned a Bachelor of Arts from California Christian College, and I now pastor a small church in Oxnard, California. I also work for the County of Ventura working with parents who are in danger of losing their children. Working to help others comes naturally when we know the Lord is in charge of our life and know that others will not have the joy we have without someone to show them the truth that Jesus Christ is alive and desires to save them. I am now working with people who many feel do not have hope or are worthy of being helped.

One of the areas I now serve the Lord in is as a member of the Oxnard Chiefs Advisory Board. I have been a member of the board for the past four years. In Oxnard we have a Police Chief, Jeri Williams, who is a Christian woman and I am blessed that she knows me not from my criminal record, but from the Godly man I now am. I serve on this board as well as being involved in other charitable endeavors throughout Ventura County. God has been merciful to me beyond comprehension, gracious beyond reason, and forgiving beyond the natural.

Jesus is the only reason and explanation for how a man with my baggage can be set free from the pain of carrying the baggage, set free from the consequences of the baggage and set free from the punishment the baggage carried. Jesus Christ also is the one who gave back what the enemy stole. One of my favorite sayings is this – WE CANNOT FIX THE PAST, BUT THROUGH JESUS HE HAS CORRECTED OUR FUTURE!!!

I am doing what I saw a man do years ago in Fresno County Jail, sharing the love of God to those who are hurting and who have been forgotten and judged unworthy by many. Chaplain Davis is a man who will always be special to me. In fact, when I was ordained in 2005, he took the time to come and be there. As I began to preach behind the pulpit, I looked out over hundreds of people. I saw family and friends, and then his beaming face caught my eyes, and I could not hold back the tears that flowed. I stepped out from the pulpit and made my way to him and threw my arms around him. Hugging him was a small way of saying, "Thanks for never giving up on me." Writing this is, I hope, another way of saying "thank you" to the greatest chaplain I know!!!

The Bible–the Book of Truth–says: **"After all, what gives us hope and joy, and what is our proud reward and crown? It is you! Yes, you will bring us much joy as we stand together before our Lord Jesus when He comes back again. For you are our pride and joy"** (First Thessalonians 2:19-20). (NLT)

Greg Runyon

- 14 -

NO MORE FAILURE

It would be great if we could say that every man or woman who professed faith in Christ as their Savior went on to live a completely changed life and never went back to the old life, but this is not true. However, it is possible, as the stories in this book prove, that one can live faithfully for Christ and be a success even if all their life they have been a failure. **You** can be a success in life.

What makes the difference? Let us see the answer in the lives of the following:

Fatman and Snake

Perhaps two men that I worked with illustrate this best–Richard and Kerry. Both Richard and Kerry would come to the office for counseling, but I got to know Richard better than Kerry. Later Richard would work with us in the jail.

Richard and Kerry were drug partners on the street but I didn't know this until several years after I had met both of them. It was Richard who first told me that he and Kerry were partners on the street. The next time I saw Kerry, in jail, I said, "I understand you and Richard were partners on the street." Kerry looked at me and said he didn't know any Richard. Suddenly he said, "Oh, you mean 'Fatman.'" I didn't know that this was Richard's street name, but it was, and Kerry's street name was "Snake."

Richard was one of the first that I began to counsel when I started to work at the jail. He would come to my office weekly and we would study together. I found out that he came from a spiritual background and that his brother was an Elder in one of the local churches.

After spending several months in jail, Richard was released. I went to his home and would have Bible study with him. But he never quite got away from the pills and the old life and he would keep coming back to jail and we would have our weekly meetings in the chaplains' office again.

When Richard was 40 years old he was arrested for what would be the last time. He later told me that when he was being booked in he called his daughter and asked her to come and bail him out. She said, "Daddy, why should I bail you out? You will just go back to jail again." Richard told her that he wouldn't because this time he was really going to commit his life to the Lord.

As I recall she did not bail him out and he stayed in jail until his trial. At his trial he was sentenced to several years in prison and it was in prison that his life really began to change. He was sent to Vacaville State Prison and there he met a man who knew of a rehab home in Texas. When Richard was released he didn't come back to Fresno, but went to the rehab home in Texas.

Richard told me that whenever he would be released from prison and return to Fresno he would be known as "Richard, the drug addict," but when he walked into the rehab home in Texas he was greeted as "Richard, our brother in Christ." Richard was in Texas for several years and even went into Huntsville Prison to minister to the inmates.

When he returned to Fresno, he contacted me and I was delighted to see his growth in the Christian life. Richard continued to do well and was active in the church where his brother was an Elder. After some time I asked Richard if he would like to come into the jail as a volunteer and work with us and he said, "Yes."

In order for someone to come in as a volunteer and work with the chaplains, they needed to go through a background check, be approved by Lieutenant Leonardo and the Captain, and then they were issued an ID card and could come into the jail.

It so happened that when Richard finished his paperwork and I went to submit it to Lieutenant Leonardo, he was on vacation and another lieutenant was in charge to grant the approval. He denied Richard's application. I well remember his words, "I wouldn't let an ex-inmate into my jail if he had six chaplains standing around him."

When Lieutenant Leonardo came back from vacation I told him what had happened. I asked if there was any way we could get Richard in as a volunteer as I was sure he would be a great asset to our core of volunteers. He said that since this other lieutenant had denied the application he would need some letters of reference for Richard in order to re-open the case. Several wrote letters highly recommending Richard and he was approved and became one of our best volunteers.

The first time Richard came in to speak at a chapel service I was with him and the topic of his talk surprised me. He talked about how one needed to develop a budget for their finances if they were going to make it on the streets. I remember him saying that when he was on drugs, if he had $100 in his pocket he would spend it that day. If he didn't have any money, he would go steal something to get money.

After he finished his talk, I saw the wisdom of what he was saying. Later, Bruce Hood would tell me the same thing, that money to an ex-addict is a great temptation. Bruce said that for four years after he became a Christian he gave all his money to his mother to manage for him. He said that with money in his pocket there was the temptation to go out and spend it and perhaps not wisely.

Later, Richard would come into the jail with a Mr. Howard Ham. Howard taught a recovery program in the jail and also had a recovery home on the streets called "Highways and Hedges." Richard also helped Howard in his rehab home and program on the streets.

Richard's health finally deteriorated and he was in a wheelchair and had a power scooter with which to get around. He used to come by our office in his scooter and we would be able to share about what the Lord was doing in his life. Then I lost track of Richard. I think he may have passed away and I was never notified. But this I know, we will meet in heaven.

Kerry was a different story.

It has been probably close to forty years since Kerry and I first sat in my office and talked about the Lord, but I still remember one thing he said. Kerry professed to be a Christian and he said one time he was talking to a friend on the streets about the Lord and was describing heaven to his friend. He said to his friend, "Man, they really know how to party up there!"

"Partying" was Kerry's downfall. He would get out of jail and go back to the same old friends and party with them and was soon back on dope and back in jail again. I don't recall how many times he was in and out of our jail, but it was quite a few times. Sometimes he would do a little prison time, but he would get out of prison, come back to Fresno and start the cycle all over again.

The last time Kerry was in our jail and was facing some prison time, Richard, "Fatman," came to see him. He told Kerry to keep in touch with him and that when Kerry was to be released from prison Richard would meet him and take him to Texas to the Recovery Home that had helped Richard change his life. Kerry promised that he would do this.

This time Kerry seemed genuinely interested and both

Richard and I thought that he would keep his promise, but when the time came for him to be released from prison he told Richard he didn't want to go to Texas, but wanted to come back to Fresno. He did come back to Fresno and in a short time he was dead from an overdose of drugs.

Two men–both had the same opportunity, one took it, the other didn't. **We are the result of our choices.** As Howard Ham used to tell the men in jail, "It's your stinking thinking that got you here." Give your life to Christ, let Him change the way you think, and you will end up like Richard with your life transformed.

As the Bible says in Romans 12:2: **"Don't copy the behavior and customs of this world, but let God transform you into a new person by changing the way you think. Then you will know what God wants you to do, and you will know how good and pleasing and perfect His will really is."** (NLT)

The Bible also talks a lot about the "two ways." Jesus said there was the "narrow way" that leads to life and the "broad way" that leads to destruction. In his gospel, John put it this way in chapter three and verse 36, **"And all who believe in God's Son have eternal life. Those who don't obey the Son will never experience eternal life, but the wrath of God remains upon them."** (NLT)

Henry – *Back Again*

In chapter two I told you about Mike, the very first inmate with whom I counseled, and how he trusted Christ as his Savior. I mentioned he had a brother Henry. Following is Henry's story.

When Henry made his commitment to Christ he did very well at first. He eventually became part of an organization that sought to help inmates and those released from prison. One of their functions was to run a rehabilitation home in

Fresno and Henry was part of the staff in the home. But Henry had a problem: he looked at other Christians and not at Christ. In the home he saw those on staff who were not really living for Christ and he became disillusioned with Christianity. If we are going to be a success as a Christian we must keep our eyes on Christ, not on other professing Christians. As the Bible says, "**...keeping our eyes on Jesus, on whom our faith depends from start to finish**" (Hebrews 12:2). (NLT)

Henry went back to using drugs. One day as he was going to buy his drugs someone told him that the drug dealer was "packing" (that is, he was carrying a gun), so Henry took a gun to the meeting. During the transaction something went wrong and Henry shot and killed the drug dealer.

Henry was brought to jail and he refused to talk to anyone. His attorney was a lady Public Defender (PD) and when he refused to see her, she knew that I knew Henry so she came to me to see if I could convince him to see her. When we went to the officer and asked if I could talk to Henry, the officer refused to let me go see him. This is the only time I ever saw a PD cry. When the officer refused to let me go and see Henry, she broke down and cried and said, "This man is facing the death penalty and Chaplain Davis needs to convince him to talk to me."

To this day I can't remember my talking to Henry, but I do recall that he did eventually talk to his PD. Henry would come to my office regularly and we would talk about Christ and his spiritual life.

He did give his life back to Christ and we would study the Bible together. Eventually he went to trial and was found guilty and sentenced to life in prison.

For many years we corresponded while he was in prison. One day his letter came back marked "deceased." Shortly after that his brother Mike called and said that Henry had a massive brain hemorrhage and died. He was only 48 years old.

If you are like Henry and think that there are too many "hypocrites" in the church, just remember, if you let a hypocrite stand between you and God, at least he is closer to God than you. The real secret is to keep your eyes on Jesus. He will never fail you and you will never be disappointed in Him. The Bible says that we run the race of life **"...by keeping our eyes on Jesus..."** (Hebrews 12:2). (NLT)

Billy – *The Struggle*

There were others who made a good start but did not finish well. I will mention only one more, because I spent years working with Billy. Only our Lord knows if Billy really knew the Lord.

Billy was another who I thought would do great as a Christian. After Billy had made a commitment to Christ in the jail, he was sentenced to four years at San Quentin. After he arrived at San Quentin the chaplain there, Chaplain Harry Howard, thought that Billy was one of the most dedicated men with whom he had ever worked.

Billy had "burned" many people on the streets and he had many enemies. Because they couldn't get to Billy they turned to his family. While Billy was in prison some of these enemies killed his 18-year-old brother. This brother was at home and out in the front yard with his mother and sister when a car pulled up in front of the house. He told his mother and sister to go inside the house and as he walked to the car he was shot and killed in cold blood.

Not only did they kill his brother but they kidnapped one of his sisters. They cut off all her hair and sexually molested her for three days before turning her loose.

When Billy was released from San Quentin, Glenn Morrison, who had a prison ministry and recovery home, took Billy into his rehab home. This was a remarkable opportunity for Billy to grow in the Christian life, but he started using even while in the home. This home was in the Bay area and when his sister in Fresno died, Billy left the home and came back to Fresno.

For the next 10 to 12 years Billy lived an up and down life. Dr. Trowbridge, one of our volunteers at the jail, got Billy a good paying job and he did good for several months but then he returned to the dope. I believe part of his problem was that he would not cut his old friends loose and they eventually got him back into drugs. As you see from Rocky's and Bruce's testimonies, we have to leave the old friends and make new friends who are good Christians.

Billy and his wife had a bad marriage. One day they got into a terrible fight and she stabbed him with a butcher knife. While he was recovering, he phoned me and asked me to come get him and take him to his father's place. He said that he was fearful that if he stayed where he was, he would be killed. So I picked him up and took him to his father's place in a town just south of Fresno.

Billy left his wife and moved in with a girl and they lived not too far from us in Fresno. I used to go out and have Bible studies with them. Shortly before I started having Bible studies with them, Billy had just gotten out of the hospital. Again, his old enemies had attacked him and beaten him and broke his jaw.

I finally convinced Billy he needed to go a rehabilitation program called "Teen Challenge," which had been started by David Wilkerson. He was high on drugs and I knew the program would not accept him in that condition, so I took him to another program called "Second Chance" and he went "cold turkey" and got off the dope. I then took him to Shafter, near Bakersfield, CA, to the Teen Challenge program.

He was accepted and was there about three weeks and doing good when his girl friend came down and persuaded him to leave and come with her. From then on he went downhill and one night when he was under the influence of drugs he was struck and killed by a car.

As I said, there were others who professed Christ as Savior but could not seem to make it on the streets. However, those who have shared their testimonies in this book are progressing in their Christian life. Most of them have been walking faithfully with Christ for 20 years or more. You CAN make it as a Christian if you put Christ first every day.

When I would counsel with the men who had trusted Christ, I would stress four things that they needed to do in order to keep living for Christ.

FOUR THINGS YOU MUST DO:

1. I told them they needed to know that when they accepted Christ as their Savior, God's Holy Spirit came to live within them and He was there to help them live for Christ (see Ephesians 1:13-14). The Holy Spirit was able to keep them from going back to the old life. They needed to learn to trust the Holy Spirit to give them strength to live for Christ and to overcome temptation (see Galatians 5:17-24).

   All Christians have the Holy Spirit in them, but not all are filled or controlled by the Holy Spirit. When we sin, His control is broken and we need to confess that sin immediately (see First John 1:9). Then we need to pray and ask the Holy Spirit to again control our lives (see First John 5:14-15). Don't start a day until you know that you have let the Holy Spirit take control of your life.

2. I told them they needed to study the Bible on a regular basis and to obey what the Bible said (see Second Timothy 2:15-19). (See also Appendix B, page 169)

3. I told them they needed to learn to pray. I told them

that prayer was just talking to God, letting God know their needs, thanking God for His help, and praying for others and asking God to help them. I encouraged them to memorize verses on prayer such as Matthew 7:7 and First John 5:14-15. There are many definitions of prayer, but one of mine is that prayer is just a child talking to their Father.

4. I told them they needed to find a church that preached the Bible and attend faithfully.

Through the years I noticed that there were, in particular, two things that drew men away from Christ. One was going back to the old gang and getting back on drugs. Bruce Hood told me that it was four years before he felt strong enough to be around his old drug buddies. Then, when he did go back and try to tell them about Christ, he found that they didn't want to hear and quickly left.

The second thing that was instrumental in drawing men away from Christ is that they would get hooked up with the wrong woman. Get strong in Christ before you begin to have any relationships with the opposite sex and then only go with a woman who is a strong Christian.

To close this chapter I asked Bruce and Rocky to share what they needed to do in order to keep from falling back into the old way of life. You have read their testimonies so you know that both of these men came from a life of drugs and crime, but for years and years they have both lived their lives for Christ and both are a tribute to the power of God to change one's life no matter what their background.

Both of them told me essentially the same thing: surround yourself with strong Christian people. Rocky mentioned how Chaplain Lile and I were of great help to him, and his pastor was also of great help to him. Both said stay away from old friends.

Rocky even had to stay away from his own family for ten years because there was so much alcohol and drugs there. They became angry with Rocky and told him that he thought he was too good for them, but with tears he would try to tell them that it was their lifestyle that kept him away because he would be tempted to go back to the old way of life. Following is what Rocky wrote:

Being a new follower of Christ I knew I had to leave the old ways behind me. I stayed away from the old friends and family and that was no cakewalk. Being around that all my life was a big test. My friends and family came against me, challenging my new faith. I had to get new friends and family in the body of Christ. Coming from a large family I now have a large Christian family to see me through my many challenges in life. No drugs, no alcohol, no gang violence—23 years now and I'm loving every day of it with Christ and my wife and kids. Thank you, Jesus!!

Bruce said that for years he never went out at night because night was when he used to do his wild living. Bruce also said that he gave all his money to his mother to keep for him because if he had money in his pocket there was the temptation to use it to do the wrong things.

Many times we are tempted by the allurements of this life, things that promise pleasure and satisfaction but in the end destroy us. One of the inmates who attended my chapel service illustrates this. I cannot recall this inmate's name, but he would come to the chapel services and one day he told me his story.

This man had made a profession of faith in Christ while doing time in prison. When he was released from prison he took his "gate" money and bought himself a pair of new Nike shoes. He said he was standing on the street corner after buying his shoes and he saw his former connection driving down the street. He said the fellow had a big luxury car, was dressed in a fine, expensive suit and he knew that on his finger was a big diamond ring and in his wallet was a lot of money. He said, "There was my connection with all these nice, expensive things and all I had was Jesus and my Nikes."

What he didn't realize was that with Jesus he had more than his connection could ever have, but he didn't see it that way and turned again to crime to satisfy his desire for "things" and ended up back in jail.

Someone has said, "If God is everything, then if we have God, we have everything."

As we close this chapter I wonder if you noticed, as I did, how the mothers of these men and women never gave up on them no matter what they did. I noticed this especially in Rocky's, Bruce's and Greg's testimonies.

We started this chapter by mentioning that some did fail, but that we don't need to. Just as in salvation Christ did everything necessary for us to be saved, we just need to believe and come to Him. It's the same with living for Christ. <u>God has done everything necessary for us to be successful in our Christian walk.</u> **"As we know Jesus better, His divine power gives us everything we need for living a godly life"** (II Peter 1:3). (NLT)

He has given us the Holy Spirit to live within us and to empower us daily. But just like salvation, we have to come to Christ daily and ask to be controlled by the Holy Spirit. Every morning commit your life anew to Christ. Confess any sin and ask the Holy Spirit to control you for that day. If you sin during the day confess it immediately and ask God to control you again with His Spirit. (See First John 1:7-9)

<u>Memorize</u> First John 1:9, Ephesians 5:18 and First John 5:14-15. By depending on the Holy Spirit daily **YOU CAN** succeed.

The Bible—the Book of Truth—says: "**...and he will**

succeed, because the Lord can make him succeed" (Romans 14:4b). (Beck's Translation, underlining mine)

"And I am sure that God, who began the good work within you, will continue His work until it is finally finished on that day when Christ Jesus comes back again" (Philippians 1:6). (NLT)

"For God is working in you, giving you the desire to obey Him and the power to do what pleases Him" (Philippians 2:13). (NLT)

- 15 -

FINAL YEARS

My wife Myrna had served as the secretary in the chaplains' office for many years, but in 2008 she retired. As she would be home alone now, I decided that I would cut my hours from five to two days a week. I talked to the jail Program Supervisor, Michele, and there was no problem. Thus began two very satisfying years to add to a very satisfying ministry.

My final two years at the jail were spent mainly in going into the pods and talking with selected individuals and in getting some men involved in studying the Bible, using an excellent study Bible put out by the Nelson Bible Company. Twelve of these Bibles were sent to me free each month by "The Living Water Project" in Glide, Oregon.

My ministry in these years was made possible for two reasons. One was Monte Byrd. Monte worked with Valley Missions and he took over the supervision of all our volunteers and he did an outstanding job. Monte's background was in the business world (he had been very successful for many years in running his own pharmacy) and he was good at organizing and in supervising personnel. He also took charge of training our new volunteers.

The other reason was that under Monte's supervision we now had volunteer chaplains to work each floor of the main jail where I had been working. Glenn R. worked the sixth floor, Knute worked the fifth floor and Galen worked floors three and four. At first I worked the infirmary on the second floor and after I retired, Galen took this over also. Knute, Glenn and Galen would go into the housing units and talk with the men. They would hand out Bibles and literature and the Gospel Echoes Bible studies and minister to the spiritual needs of the inmates. These men were some of our finest volunteers.

As I said, each month 12 of the Nelson Study Bibles were sent to me free. Now my problem was how to see that these Bibles were given to men who would really use them. All the inmates wanted one (inmates want anything that is free!), but I knew that many of them would not use them. I had promised those who sent me the Bibles that I would do my best to see that only men who would really use them would get a copy. So I had to devise a way to find out who was really serious about studying the Bible.

When an inmate would request a copy of the Nelson Bible I would go to his housing unit and talk with him. If I felt he was genuine in his desire to study the Bible I would have him do two things: one, I asked him to write out his testimony. I explained to him that a testimony covered three areas: what his life was like before he received Christ as his Savior, how he came to know Christ, and what his life has been like since he started following Christ.

The second thing that I asked them to do was to read the Gospel of John. This was a special edition of John, with notes, put out by the same people who sent me the Nelson Study Bible. It is the best edition of the Gospel of John that I have seen in my 70 years of Christian experience. In Appendix C (page 172) I tell you how you can get your own free copy.

In the *Introductory Notes* at the beginning of this Gospel of John the inmate would read about LIFE'S MOST IMPORTANT QUESTION. **"WHAT MUST I DO TO HAVE ETERNAL LIFE?"** That's the most important question you will ever ask. As you read through this Gospel you will find that eternal life comes not by doing, but by believing: **"... anyone who believes in Me already has eternal life"** (John

6:47). (NLT) Get this Gospel and read it (see Appendix D, page 174).

Throughout the pages of this special edition of John's Gospel there are many footnotes which help one understand what it means to believe and then there are Concluding Notes which review what it means to believe and what to do after one accepts Christ as one's Savior.

As the inmate read the Gospel of John, I asked him to underline the word "Believe" and the word "Life" and then write down how many times he found each. In all the answers I don't think I ever got two that had the same number! Also, I asked the inmate to write down each of the seven miracles that John recorded and where they were found.

After receiving back their testimony and their answers to the questions on John (which usually took several days), I would again call on the inmate and go over his testimony and his answers with him. I wish that I had kept these testimonies as I would have printed some of them here as they were very good. One inmate sent me four pages written on both sides!

Once I was convinced that they would really use the Study Bible, I would give them their copy. With it I included two pages of notes. One page would explain how to use the Nelson Study Bible and the other page how to study a book of the Bible.

On the page on how to use the Study Bible I pointed out that there were many good features about this Study Bible but that probably the two most important were the notes on each page and the Subject Index at the back of the Bible. The Subject Index covered many subjects, but I would have them start with the subject of "Salvation." Under this subject there were verses on salvation, word studies on various words related to salvation and a chart showing the key words of salvation.

On the page on how to study a Book of the Bible I showed them how to take their new Bible and answer the five "**W**'s."

FIVE W'S:

"**W**ho" wrote the book?

"**W**hen" was the book written (that is, the "date" of the writing)?

"**W**hy" was it written (the theme of the book)?

"To **W**hom" was it written (the recipients of the letter)?

"**W**here" was it written (where was the author when he wrote the book, for example, some of Paul's letters were written from prison)?

One inmate wrote me after receiving his Bible and said that he had been reading the Bible for several years but could not understand it. He said he had learned more in one week with this Study Bible then he had in all the previous years of reading the Bible on his own.

Another "tool" that I used in these years was *THE NEW BELIEVERS BIBLE: NEW TESTAMENT.* Many times I would give this to an inmate if I felt he was not ready for the Study Bible. I found this New Testament to be excellent in helping new believers get started and keep growing in the Christian life.

FIVE PARTS TO THIS NEW TESTAMENT:

1. **"How You Can Know God;"**
2. **"Cornerstones"**– basic Christian beliefs;
3. **"First Steps"**– what one needs to begin with as a new Christian, such as study the Bible, pray, look for and attend the right church, obey God, etc.;
4. **"Off and Running"**– how to keep growing as a Christian;
5. **"How to Study the Bible."** See Appendix C (page 172) on where to order this New Testament.

Brandon – *A Chance to Witness*

My last few years at the jail I spent a lot of time with two particular inmates. One was Brandon Leon LeBar and the other was Robert.

When Brandon was arrested his left leg had been severely injured and it had to be amputated, so he spent all of his time while in jail in the main jail infirmary. Brandon had known the Lord before his arrest, but like Monty Christensen he had gotten out of fellowship, back into crime and was arrested.

In jail, Brandon got his life back into fellowship with the Lord and two things impressed me about Brandon. One was his desire to know the Word of God and the other was his desire that others would come to know Christ.

When I would call on Brandon, we would spend time discussing various Bible passages. He always had a lot of questions about what he had been reading in the Bible. Also, he became a great lover of J. Vernon McGee who had a Bible teaching ministry on the radio. Dr. McGee had been one of my teachers at Biola many years before and I had some of his books which I shared with Brandon. Eventually, a dear friend of his and a sister in the Lord had the publishers send him several volumes of Dr. McGee's "Through the Bible," a study of each book of the Bible.

Brandon was in a room with three other men and as one man would be released another would take his place. Brandon began to witness to them and several of these men came to faith in Christ.

Then something happened which I had never in all my 34 years at the jail seen happen. The officers allowed Brandon to go to some of the other rooms in the infirmary and witness to those men. Many of these men also made a profession of faith in Christ.

There was one room in the infirmary (sometimes more) where female inmates were housed and Brandon was even allowed to witness to them. He could not go into the room with the women, but the officers would place him in a vacant room next to them and he would speak to them through the wall. Brandon liked to "rap" and he would "rap" the gospel to them. (You can view two of his raps on You Tube by searching, "Thank You Lord," and/or "Let this be done.")

Brandon left for prison shortly before I retired but we still correspond. He was in our jail for 27 months and he told me that in that time the Lord had given him one soul per month. God used him to bring 27 people to profess faith in Christ.

As I write this Brandon has been in prison for around six years and he is still going strong with the Lord. Brandon is still witnessing to men and leading them to Christ. Recently he wrote me and shared a letter with me from another inmate in which this inmate expressed his thanks to Brandon for leading him to Christ.

In his last letter Brandon sent me a letter written by the chaplain at the prison where Brandon is serving his time. He tells how Brandon is an active participant in their Sunday service and then he says this:

"I have had the pleasure of knowing and interacting with him (Brandon) on many occasions other than our Sunday services and I have seen him grow and mature spiritually into the man he is today. Brandon is a kind and respectful man and possesses a positive attitude that always affects those around him. He is considerate and very well liked and respected amongst his peers."

He also mentions that Brandon is a volunteer member of *The Urban Ministry Institute*, which is a program designed to equip men for Christian Leadership ministry. He concludes by saying that Brandon leads the weekly Bible study program because of his ability to correctly communicate the teachings of the Bible.

Robert – *Still in the Word*

Robert, the other one who I worked closely with in my last few years at the jail, was in our jail for five years awaiting trial. Robert was led to profess Christ as his Savior by Monte, the one who trained our volunteers. At first, Monte would counsel with Robert one week and I would meet one-on-one with Robert the next week. However, Monte became ill and I began to counsel with Robert on a weekly basis. This was a great blessing to me as I enjoyed working with Robert.

Each week we would talk about what Robert was going through and we would study a chapter of the Bible. Each week as Robert left I would give him a list of questions based on the Bible chapter we would be studying the next week. Robert was an excellent student and he would always get an "A" on his study paper.

Before Robert would go back to his room he always wanted me to tell him a joke. No problem, except that Robert was there for five years waiting to go to trial and after two years I ran out of jokes! I tried repeating jokes, but he would quickly tell me, " Chaplain, you told me that before."

Robert was still in jail when I retired, but several months after I left the jail he was sentenced to prison. Robert and I corresponded after I left the jail and when he arrived at prison, we continued to write each other. He asked if we could continue our Bible studies by mail. I send Robert a chapter of the Bible to read and include questions for him to answer. As this is being written we have concluded a study in the Gospel of St. Mark and I Thessalonians and are starting a study in the Gospel of John.

Retirement

Finally, when I neared eighty years of age, I realized that it was time to retire and move to Southern California where we could be near our son, Brent. So I went to Michele and told her I was going to retire at the end of 2010.

It was hard to say goodbye to many of these officers as I had worked with them for many years. One big male officer had tears in his eyes as we said goodbye. One of our lady sergeants told me she would not say goodbye because she would burst into tears if she did.

My last day at the jail was a memorable one. Usually when someone retired who had been at the jail as long I had, they were given some sort of going away party, but I told Michele that I didn't want any such party. Thus, I thought my last day at the jail would just be going around and saying good-bye and fading off quietly into the sunset.

One of the officers with whom I worked for almost 30 years was Captain Weldon. I first knew her as an officer, then she made sergeant and lieutenant, and for the past several years before I retired she was one of the captains at the jail. She was one of our finest officers.

Captain Weldon had been on vacation my last week at the jail, but on my last day she returned and one of the officers said that she wanted to see me. Thinking it was just to say goodbye, I went to her office to say farewell. I chatted with her for a while and also with Della, the captain's secretary, whom I had also known for many years. Both of these gals were super to work with and it was great to visit with them both, though sad to say goodbye.

As I was about to leave, Captain Weldon said, "Come with me." She took me to a conference room where about 30 officers and civilian staff had assembled to send me off, including Rocky, whose testimony you have read. Even our sheriff, Sheriff Mims, was there, which was quite an honor. What a wonderful surprise this was and I will always remember the love shown to me. There was a cake and they had made a special scrapbook for me which I cherish, as it had pictures of all the sheriffs I had served under plus one of

Chaplain Knight and many of the officers who I had worked with through the years. These wonderful people also gave me a card with a generous love-gift in it.

When inmates would describe how they left the jail for prison they would say, "I rolled up and caught the bus." Finally I "rolled up," caught the "bus" (my car), and headed for home and retirement.

The Bible verse that, to me, best describes my jail ministry, is I Thessalonians 2:19-20: **"For what is our hope or joy or crown of rejoicing? Are not even ye in the presence of our Lord Jesus Christ at His coming? For ye are our glory and joy."** (KJV) That will be a glorious day when we stand before Jesus with those who are there because we were faithful in service and in prayer.

Jesus is coming; are you ready? Along with those who came to faith in Christ at the Fresno County Jail, I hope to see hundreds more of you who have come to faith in Christ as you have read this book. Write us!

As we close this book let me close with some of the greatest verses from the Bible—the Book of Truth: **"...God is love. God showed how much He loved us by sending His only Son into the world so that we might have eternal life through Him. This is real love. It is not that we loved God, but that He loved us and sent His Son as a sacrifice to take away our sins"** (First John 4:8b-10). (NLT)

"For God so loved the world that He gave his only Son, so that everyone who believes in Him will not perish but have eternal life" (John 3:16). (NLT)

EPILOGUE

Dear Reader,

Have you had a Life-Changing Encounter with the Lord Jesus Christ? If it came about through the reading of this book, I would love to hear from you. For contact information see Appendix D, page 174.

If you have not yet made that commitment to Christ as your Lord and Savior, I trust you will do it soon. Read again the testimonies in this book, and the message and God's plan of salvation in God's Plan, Appendix A, page 165.

The stories you have read are true encounters with the Living God. No matter who you are or what you have done, or what your present or past is, God can change you.

Once you make Christ your Lord and Savior by faith, write Gospel Echoes and get your free Bible studies. Also, write Living Waters and get the free Gospel of John (see Appendix D, page 174). Lastly, read Appendix B beginning on page 169 and start to read the Bible.

Thank you for reading this book. My prayer for the book is that it helps those who do not know Christ as their Lord and Savior, and encourages and strengthens those who do know Him as Lord and Savior.

Would you promise to pray this prayer daily when possible: "Lord, touch someone today as they read Chaplain Davis's book." Please let us know of your commitment by writing us at Gospel Echoes Team.

Finally, if you would like to make a donation so this book can be given free to inmates, send a check to:

Gospel Echoes Team - P. O. Box 555
Goshen, Indiana 46527-0555

Tell them you want it to go to the fund to print the "Glenn Davis Jail Book." One hundred percent of what you send will be used to provide this book free to inmates.

APPENDIX A
GOD'S PLAN

God has a wonderful plan and it includes **you**! God's plan is to bring you to Himself and the Bible says that God had this plan before He created the world, **"...even before He made the world, God loved us and chose us in Christ to be holy and without fault in His eyes"** (Ephesians 1:4). (NLT) The Bible says God's plan is "unchanging." **"His unchanging plan has always been to adopt us into His own family by bringing us to Himself through Jesus Christ..."** (Ephesians 1:5). (NLT)

Think of it, before God even thought about creating the universe, He thought about you! And He is still thinking about you. Why? Because He loves you. Why does He love you? Man, I don't know, but He loves you. I don't know why He loves me, but He does.

James says in James 1:18 that God, **"...chose to make us His own children...and we...became His choice possession."** Matthew Henry, in his commentary, says this means, "God's portion and treasure." God thinks about you as His treasure. We are talking here about GOD, the God of the universe, the Almighty God who created everything. He wants YOU. Please, please understand how much God wants you to be His child and how much HE LOVES YOU.

But there was a problem. God knew we would rebel against Him and become self-centered, and that our sin would have to be dealt with, so <u>before</u> He created the world He planned that Jesus would come and die on the cross to save us, and Jesus was willing to come. (First Peter 1:20; Revelation 13:8).

So the story of the Bible is God focusing on one thing, His plan to bring you into His family. In Genesis chapter three we have sin entering the world, and God's first promise that He will send the "seed of the woman" (which refers to Jesus) to "crush the serpent's head." This is a graphic picture of Jesus conquering Satan and sin.

Then God chooses Abraham (Genesis chapter 12:1-3) and promises to bless all mankind through Abraham's descendents. Bible scholars believe this is a reference to Jesus, and that through Him it would be possible for all to become part of God's family.

Roughly a thousand years later, God promised David (II Samuel 7) that the Messiah (Jesus) would come through David's line. At one time, there was only one little baby left of David's line as the wicked Queen Athaliah killed all of her grandsons, except one, who was hidden away by his aunt (II Kings 11:1-3).

But God's plan and purpose prevailed and finally Jesus came. John says that Jesus was God (John 1:1) and that He became a man (John 1:14). The four Gospels (Matthew, Mark, Luke and John) record His life and how He died on the cross to pay for our sins (Mark 10:45). They tell us He was raised from the dead on the third day (I Corinthians 15:4), ascended into heaven, and will return some day (Acts 1:11).

Why did God do all of this? He did it so that you could become part of his family and live with Him forever. This was God's plan from eternity. Why did God want you to be part of His family and live with Him forever? Because HE LOVES YOU. John 3:16 says, **"For God so loved the world, that He gave His only begotten Son, that whosoever believeth in Him should not perish, but have everlasting life."** (KJV)

The Bible also says, **"God showed how much He loved us by sending His only Son into the world so that we might have eternal life through Him. This is real love. It is not that we loved God, but that He loved us and sent His Son as a sacrifice to take away our sins"** (First John 4:9-10). (NLT)

GOD IS LOVE and GOD LOVES YOU!

If you have never come to God by trusting Jesus, come to Him now. Jesus says if you come, *He will never reject you,* Saint John chapter 6 and verse 37. See the verses on the "Steps to Becoming God's Child" and come to Jesus now.

If you are already His child, reach out to others as God has reached out to you.

If you want further help, send for a <u>free</u> copy of the Gospel of John to:

> The Living Water Project
> P. O. Box 2
> Glide, Oregon 97443

STEPS TO BECOMING GOD'S CHILD

1. Recognize that you have sinned (Romans 3:23), and be willing to turn from your sin (Romans 2:4).
2. Realize that God loves you and that Christ has already paid the penalty for all your sins (Romans 5:8).
3. Realize that there are two destinies in life:
   a. The "wages of sin," which is "death" – eternal separation from God.
   b. The "gift of God," which is "eternal life" – forever with God.
   Notice: we earn death, but eternal life is a gift. This gift is "through Jesus Christ our Lord." Jesus has paid for the "gift" and God now offers you eternal life – FREE! We choose which destiny is ours by making Jesus Christ our Lord (Romans 10:9-10).
4. To accept Jesus Christ as your Lord means that you are willing to turn from your sin and to follow and obey Christ the rest of your life.

5. To do this you must believe that God raised Jesus from the dead and then confess that He is your Lord and Savior.

6. You may pray a prayer something like this: "Lord Jesus, I realize that I am a sinner and that the wages of sin is death. But I believe you love me and that you paid for all my sins on the Cross and that you rose from the dead. I now turn from my sin and ask you to forgive me. I want to live the rest of my life for You."

7. Recognize God's promise that you are saved (Romans 10:13).

HOW TO STUDY THE BIBLE

The Bible was difficult for many of the inmates to understand. We would always give them a modern version of the Bible because the King James Version was like Greek to them. Even so they had difficulty in understanding it, so I gave them the following method to help them as they read the Bible.

As they read the Bible I told them to look for three things: **T**ruth, **O**rders, **P**romises, and at the end of the chapter to make a **S**ummary. This spells **TOPS**.

T.O.P.S.

TRUTH: Truth is simply a statement of fact. The best definition I ever heard of truth came from an inmate. Once in a chapel service I asked the question, "What is truth?" After several had replied one inmate said, "Truth is reality." That is exactly what "truth" is, it is REALITY. The Bible is a book of Truth – read it, study it and find out what is real.

ORDERS: Orders are simply commands, but I used "orders" because I wanted to spell TOPS. Every order God gives is for our good. To obey God is to do the best thing you can for yourself.

PROMISES: Look for any promise from God. There are two kinds of promises in the Bible: "conditional," that is, there is something you must do to claim the promise. The other kind of promise is "unconditional." God simply says, "I am going to do this," and He does it. Be sure you note what kind of promise the promise is that you discover.

SUMMARY: After you finish the chapter, look at the "truths" you have found, look at the "orders" and the "promises." Are you believing the truth? Are you obeying the order? Are you claiming the promise? Write down what you learned from this chapter and what God has led you to do as a result of your study.

Some of the men wanted to study the Bible with others in their pod, so I gave them the following outline. I told them that they should agree to read a certain chapter and that before they met, each one should study the chapter and then they would share what they had learned. The following was the outline I told them to use in their study.

The outline followed the letters of the alphabet so it was easy for them to remember it. There were six steps to the study.

SIX STEPS TO STUDY THE BIBLE

A title: They were to give the chapter a title, something that would help them to remember what the chapter was about. This is one of the most difficult parts of the study and I told them if they had trouble coming up with a title to just skip it.

Best verse: They were to pick the verse in the chapter that meant the most to them and tell why they picked this verse.

Challenge: As they read the chapter they were to write down what challenged them in the chapter. This could be a certain verse or just a general teaching in the chapter.

Difficulties: If there was something they didn't understand in the chapter, they could share what it was. Perhaps someone else in the group could explain it to them.

Eminent Truth(s): What particular truth did they learn from the chapter? Jot it down with the verse or verses that taught this truth. There may be several truths that they would like to share. This is one of the most important parts of the study. Learn what God says in the Bible, believe it, and apply it to your life.

Final Study: After they had finished studying the chapter they were to make a summary. This could be a summary of what the chapter taught or how they were going to apply to their lives what the chapter taught.

Some Final Thoughts on Bible Study:

If you can, get a study Bible with helps. I like the Life Application Bible in the New Living Translation. One that we used a lot in the jail was the New King James Study Bible published by Nelson Publishers.

<u>Start</u> with the New Testament. The New Testament is about Jesus and how God wants us to live today.

<u>Send</u> for the Gospel of John (see Appendix D, page 174) and read it, or just read the Gospel of John in whatever edition of the Bible you have.

Next, <u>read</u> the Gospel of Mark.

Now, <u>read</u> what are called "The Prison Letters." These were written by the Apostle Paul when he was imprisoned in Rome: Ephesians, Philippians, Colossians and Philemon.

Now, <u>read</u> the Gospel of Luke and the Acts of the Apostles, both written by Luke.

Now, <u>read</u> the rest of Paul's letters: Romans, Galatians, First and Second Corinthians, First and Second Thessalonians, First Timothy, Titus, and the last book Paul wrote, Second Timothy.

<u>Read</u> the Gospel of Matthew.

<u>Finish reading</u> the New Testament starting with the book of Hebrews, then James, First and Second Peter, First, Second, and Third John, Jude and Revelation.

There are 260 chapters in the New Testament. If you read one chapter each day you will finish in about nine months.

A WORD TO CHAPLAINS AND VOLUNTEERS

What a great ministry and opportunity you have. It is my sincere wish that you may have been helped by something you have read in this book. If nothing more, I trust you have been encouraged to see how our Great God can change anyone who sincerely comes to Him with true faith in our Lord Jesus Christ.

As I write this, I am eighty-six years of age, but if I were still in Fresno, I would still be going into the jail to minister. However, as I look back there are three things that I would do if I were still in the chaplain's ministry today.

FOCUS ON MINISTRY

First, **Personal Bible Study.** I would continue the emphasis we had on getting inmates into personal Bible study, using the Gospel Echoes series of Bible studies. Glendon Bender, of Gospel Echoes, once told me that we used more of their Bible studies at Fresno County Jail than any other jail or prison that they ministered to and they minister to some 700 facilities.

Second, **Make Disciples.** I would do more to make disciple-makers out of those who came to faith in Christ. My discipleship class was a help here, but my main emphasis was on how to study the Bible and how to live the Christian life. These are surely needed, but we need to add a third, helping those who find Christ win and disciple others.

Since my retirement (that is a misnomer since I am still working for the Lord Jesus) I have read a powerful book, T4T, which means Training for Trainers. The book is written by Steve Smith with Ying Kai, a Chinese brother. This book can be purchased on Amazon. I got mine on my Kindle for 99 cents.

Ying was sent to a city of 20 million people in China and told to start a Church Planting Movement. Read the book to see how he did it, and how in a ten-year span 1,738,143 people came to faith in Christ and 158,994 churches were started (mostly house churches).

Brothers and sisters, we could empty our jails and prisons if we could have the same success. Why can't we? We have the same God. Read the book and start making not just disciples, but disciple-makers.

Third, Pray. I would pray more and teach those who I worked with how to pray. Read the following verses on prayer by the Lord Jesus: Matthew 7:7-8, 21:22; Mark 11:22-25; John 14:13-14, 15:7-8, 16:23-24. Notice that in every one of these verses Jesus says we can pray and EXPECT AN ANSWER. Meditate on these verses; believe these verses.

John, the Apostle of Love, said, **"And we will receive from Him whatever we ask because we obey Him and do the things that please Him"** (First John 3:22). (NLT) See also First John 3:23-24 and First John 5:14-15.

Ponder the following from Andrew Murray, one of my favorite authors: "As we give ourselves to intercession we shall have more and mightier conversions. Let us plead for this. The Church exists with the divine purpose and promise of conversions. Plead for the salvation of sinners."

Another excellent book on prayer, besides Andrew Murray's, "With Christ in the School of Prayer," is S. D. Gordon's book, "Quiet Talks on Prayer." This is free on Amazon Kindle.

APPENDIX D
Write for Further Spiritual Help

FREE Bible Studies:
>   Gospel Echoes Team
>   P. O. Box 555
>   Goshen, Indiana 46527-0555

FREE Living Water - The Gospel of John
>   The Living Water Project
>   P. O. Box 2
>   Glide, Oregon 97443

THE NEW BELIEVERS BIBLE NEW TESTAMENT:
>   **To purchase a copy, write:**
>   BIBLES AT COST
>   22 Blake Avenue
>   Corralitos, CA 95076.

Bruce Hood
>   Feed My Sheep Ministries
>   4239 N. Gilroy Avenue
>   Fresno, CA 93722

Ron Climer
>   Changing Lives Resource Center
>   875 West Ashlan, Suite 103
>   Clovis, California 93612

Discipleship Resources:

> The Navigators
> 3820 N. 30th Street
> Colorado Springs, CO 80904

(Disclaimer: The views presented in this book are those of the author and those he ministered to and do not necessarily represent the views of the Navigators.)

Contact the Author:

If you wish to contact Chaplain Davis or any of those who shared their testimonies in this book, you may contact them at:

> Chaplain Glenn E. Davis
> c/o Gospel Echoes Team
> P. O. Box 555
> Goshen, Indiana 46527
>
> www.gospelechoes.com

Sponsor a Book:

If you would like to make a donation so this book can be given free to inmates, designate it "Chaplain Davis Book" and send your gift to:

> Gospel Echoes Team
> P. O. Box 555
> Goshen, Indiana 46527

About The Author

Chaplain Davis is a real Californian. Not only was he born in California, at Fortuna in Humboldt County in 1930, but his great-grandmother was a California Native American, a member of the Mattolle Tribe.

Glenn was raised in Humboldt County. His early years were spent in Larabee Valley and Bridgeville. He attended Fortuna Union High School, from which he graduated in 1948. After graduation he left Humboldt to attend the Bible Institute of Los Angeles (BIOLA) in Los Angeles, California. In more recent years, Humboldt County has become known for the raising of marijuana. Little did Glenn realize that when he left Humboldt the whole county would go to pot!

Glenn graduated from Biola in 1951, and it was here that he met his wife, Myrna Maxwell, who was also a student at Biola. They were married in 1952 and had their only child, a son, Brent, born in 1955.

In 1956, Glenn and Myrna left for Washington State where they served for several months as rural missionaries until Glenn was called to pastor the Little Stone Church in Chelan, Washington. This was the first of three pastorates for Glenn. He also served churches in Roseburg and Portland, Oregon, from 1960 to 1974.

After moving to Fresno, California, Glenn became a chaplain at the Fresno County Jail where he served for 34 years. As he says, "My best years were spent in jail!"

Glenn and Myrna have two married granddaughters, Kristi Lochala and Justine Denson. They have one grandson, Austin, who is a student at Wheaton College in Illinois. They have two great-granddaughters, Elianna and Mia Lochala. They have one great-grandson, Isaiah Paul. If he lives up to that name, what a powerhouse for God he will be!

Chaplain and Mrs. Davis (around 1981)